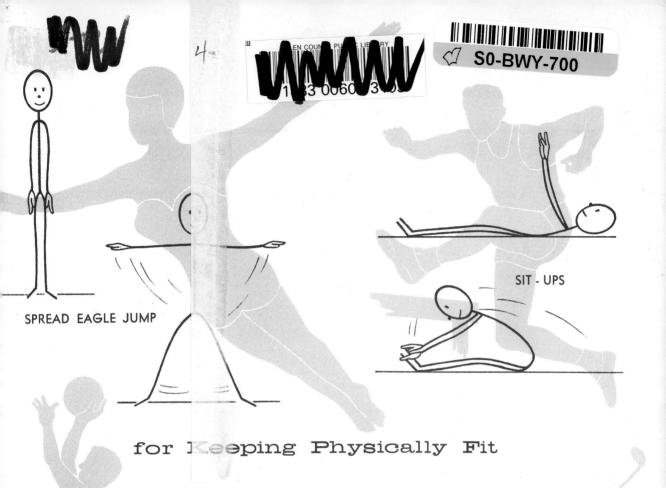

SPREAD EAGLE JUMP

SIT - UPS

for Keeping Physically Fit

LEG LIFT

WALK A MILE

CROSS TOE TOUCH

A Presidential Message

TO THE SCHOOLS
ON THE PHYSICAL FITNESS OF YOUTH

The strength of our democracy is no greater than the collective well-being of our people. The vigor of our country is no stronger than the vitality and will of all our countrymen. The level of physical, mental, moral and spiritual fitness of every American citizen must be our constant concern.

The need for increased attention to the physical fitness of our youth is clearly established. Although today's young people are fundamentally healthier than the youth of any previous generation, the majority have not developed strong, agile bodies. The softening process of our civilization continues to carry on its persistent erosion.

It is of great importance, then, that we take immediate steps to ensure that every American child be given the opportunity to make and keep himself physically fit—fit to learn, fit to understand, to grow in grace and stature, to fully live.

In answering this challenge, we look to our schools and colleges as the decisive force in a renewed national effort to strengthen the physical fitness of youth. Many of our schools have long been making strenuous efforts to assist our young people attain and maintain health and physical fitness. But we must do more. We must expand and improve our health services, health education and physical education. We must increase our facilities and the time devoted to physical activity. We must invigorate our curricula and give high priority to a crusade for excellence in health and fitness.

To members of school boards, school administrators, teachers and pupils themselves, I am directing this urgent call to strengthen all programs which contribute to the physical fitness of our youth. I strongly urge each school to adopt the three specific recommendations of my Council on Youth Fitness:

1. Identify the physically underdeveloped pupil and work with him to improve his physical capacity.

2. Provide a minimum of fifteen minutes of vigorous activity every day for all pupils.

3. Use valid fitness tests to determine pupils' physical abilities and evaluate their progress.

The adoption of these recommendations by our schools will ensure the beginning of a sound basic program of physical developmental activity.

In our total fitness efforts the schools, of course, will not stand alone. I urge that in all communities there be more coordination between the schools and the community, parents, educators and civic-minded citizens in carrying forward a resourceful, vigorous program for physical fitness—a program that will stir the imagination of our youth, calling on their toughest abilities, enlisting their greatest enthusiasm—a program which will enable them to build the energy and strength that is their American heritage.

JOHN F. KENNEDY

Track
and
Field

CES

Creative
Sports Series

BASEBALL

FOOTBALL

BASKETBALL

TRACK AND FIELD

GOLF

SWIMMING

TENNIS

ARCHERY

BADMINTON

BOWLING

CANOEING

HANDBALL

FIGURE SKATING

SKIING

TABLE TENNIS

VOLLEY BALL

WATER SKIING

Physical Fitness Program

TRACK AND FIELD

by

Earl "Bud" Myers

CROSS COUNTRY AND TRACK COACH
MANKATO STATE COLLEGE
MANKATO, MINNESOTA

and

Rich Hacker

TRACK AND FIELD COACH
BERKELEY HIGH SCHOOL
BERKELEY, CALIFORNIA

ADVISORY EDITORS

W. J. McConnell, COMMISSIONER, OHIO HIGH
SCHOOL ATHLETIC ASSOCIATION, COLUMBUS, OHIO

Cliff Harper, EXECUTIVE SECRETARY, ALABAMA
HIGH SCHOOL ATHLETIC ASSOCIATION, MONTGOMERY,
ALABAMA

James L. Pursell, VAN NUYS JUNIOR HIGH SCHOOL,
VAN NUYS, CALIFORNIA

CREATIVE EDUCATIONAL SOCIETY, Inc., Mankato, Minnesota

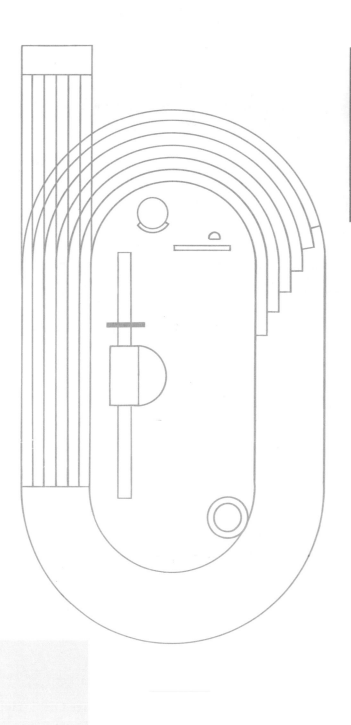

Foreword

FROM EARLY PRE-SCHOOL years onward, youngsters crawled, walked, ran, hurdled and jumped in some form or fashion, without regard to location.

Track and field events can be traced back to the pre-Christian Era when running and jumping was necessary to everyday living. It gained impetus in the hero worship days of the Greeks, was carried on by the Romans and is now participated in by practically all nations at the Olympics.

Whether or not he or she becomes a champion, all students should have the opportunity to engage in a sport which is an outlet for much pent-up energy.

In many of our elementary and secondary schools, due to lack of funds, track and field events are not taught by professionally trained instructors but by individuals whose main task is academic rather than sports.

This book was prepared for use by students who have the inherent desire to engage in track and field activities on an intra-mural basis and for others who are required to teach the sport although their training has been limited.

Of course, it will prove most useful to coaches of the sport who want it used as supplemental instructional material for youngsters who cannot get professional supervision but are above average in their track and field ability.

To all individuals, students, adults, recreational club members, camp leaders and others, this book, through its coaching hints, instruction on proper fundamentals and techniques, functional organization, practical and excellent illustrations, will help develop natural ability and knowledge of all track and field events.

J. OLIVER JACKSON
Track Coach
Abilene Christian College
Abilene, Texas

7

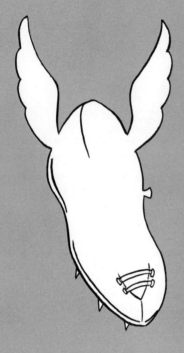

Contents

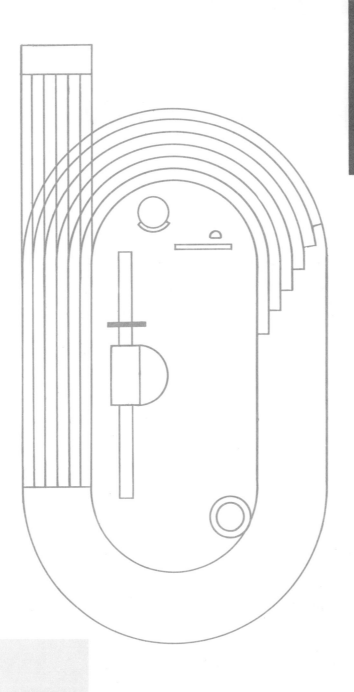

Introduction

THE YOUNG MAN and young woman who want to compete in track and field have so much to learn and usually so little time to learn it in. The coach, of course, will do everything possible within the allotted practice hours to help any youngster with a competitive desire and willingness to absorb instructions. The youngster, too, must have that inherent willingness to help himself.

This volume was developed as an instructional aid for the youngster who is serious about improving his athletic abilities and making the most of them. He does not need a coach to interpret the instructions, fundamentals and techniques listed within these pages and he will acquire knowledge which can only help him gain the goals he is seeking.

Track and Field is one sport where the participant is very often on "center stage." A hurdler receives no help when he flies over the obstacles. A sprint man cannot look to a teammate to push him closer to the finish line. A javelin thrower stands alone when he picks up his spear and starts his run toward the take-off point. Although a winning point total is accomplished through the combined efforts of each member on the team, the athlete, to be victorious, must make use of knowledge gained from his coach, his own abilities, and such information ac-

quired from this book.

Baseball, basketball or football teams can win despite shortcomings by individual members on the team. This does not hold true in track and field where competitors in most instances are pitted against each other and individual skills are of vital importance.

The student who is athletically inclined and desires to further his education by enrolling in a college of his choice will find inter-scholastic athletics an important foundation towards this achievement. The track and field training program helps him to be industrious and faithful and gives the student a solid understanding in the basic techniques of the sport. From this book, a youngster interested in furthering his knowledge of track and field, will do so absorbing the techniques and skills so simply developed.

Track and field is a unique outlet to rid oneself of excess pent-up energy. Throwing the javelin, broad jumping and running against a friendly but fleet colleague are harmless and healthy means of releasing such energy.

It is unnecessary to be outstanding in track and field, or for that matter in any other sport. The main thing is to play at something to the best of one's ability. As a participant in sports, youth will be enriched. As a spectator, a knowledge of sports, in this book, track and field, will make one a more informed individual.

Earl "Bud" Myers

EARL "BUD" MYERS
Mankato State College
Mankato, Minnesota

PICTURE ACKNOWLEDGMENTS

To the following individuals and organizations our thanks for permitting the use of pictures and illustrations in their possession.

Esquire Magazine
Library of Congress
Yale University Library
New York Public Library
J. H. Whitney

Whitney Museum of Art
Rhode Island School of Design
The Bettmann Archive
John and Alice Durant
Frank J. Basloe

Sources of pictures with page reference listed below

A.S. U.C.L.A. News Bureau 202, 205
Baldwin Wallace
   College .... (above, right) 228
John Biehl 29, 30, 31, 45, 46,
   67, 70, 103, 128, 139, 141, 150, 151,
                 160, 187
Boston U ....(below, right) 227
Canham, Don 67, 68, 69, 78, 79,
   80, 90, 91, 92, 93, 104, 105, 116, 117,
   130, 131, 142, 143, 144, 145, 152, 153,
            163, 164, 165
Chicago Daily News 134, 135
Clanton III 100
Fresno State College (above, right) 229
International News Service 72
Lloyd Jones Studio 29, 30, 31,
                   36, 37
KELO-TV News 188
N.A.I.A. 182, 183, 184, 185
Ohio State U .. 201, (below, left) 229
Schick, Jules 224
Sports Illustrated 195
Stanford U ....(above, left) 227, 244
Texas A & M 230

Track & Field News ....(below) 48,
           76, 99, 108, 111
Illinois, U of 112, 113, 114, 115,
           (above, left) 231
U.P.I. 248
Kansas, U of 226
Minnesota, U of 203
U.S. Marines, Quantico,
   Va. ....(below) 168
Wide World 25, 26, 32, 34, 35,
   (above) 38, 39, 40, 41, 42, 47, 49, 50,
   51, 52, 53, 54, 55, 56, 57, 58, 59, 60,
   62, 63, 64, 71, 74, 81, 82, 83, 84, 85,
   86, 89, 95, 96, 97, 106, 107, 118, 119,
   120, 121, 122, 123, 124, 125, 126, 129,
   132, 133, 136, 137, 138, 140, 146, 147,
   148, 154, 155, 156, 157, 158, 159, 166,
   167, (above) 168, 169, 170, 171, 172,
   175, 176, 177, 178, 179, 180, 192, 199,
   200, 204, 207, 208, 209, 210, 211, 213,
   220, 221, 222, 223, (below, left) 228,
   (below, right) 231, 246, 247, 249,
                250, 251

COLOR PLATES

"Split-Second Victory" (p. 32A)
"Clearing the First Hurdle" (p. 80A)
"Vaulter Viewing the Trip Down"
   (p. 128A)

"Coiled for the Throw" (p. 160A)
"The Shot Is Fired" (p. 192A)
"Flying Over the Bar" (p. 224A)

Full-color illustrations were rendered especially for the
CREATIVE SPORTS SERIES

Track
and
Field

How It Started

THE BIRTH OF TRACK and field events as we know them today, occurred at the dawn of earliest civilization when man obeyed a basic urge — the instinct of self-preservation.

When the pre-historic beasts attacked, there was very little man and his family could do except run. And they ran for their lives. The speedy escaped. The slow afoot didn't. Parents encouraged their children to run fast. They held races so the youngsters could develop the running ability which someday might save their lives.

As man began to triumph over animal, human dignity asserted itself. He consid-ered it an insult to keep running from animals. Resentment boiled inside him and he decided to do something about the situation.

Stones were the first lethal weapons used to kill marauding monsters. Later, as civilization progressed, crude imple-ments were fashioned into raw weapons and became even more effective devices to maintain control over animals. As the technique for throwing for accuracy and distance increased, each village boasted of a hard-throwing hunter and competi-tion began early to find out which village had the best hunter of all.

15

Early athletes getting in some vital practice. This spear-like instrument
used for protection and meat-procurement was not unlike today's javelin.

Jumping and vaulting were the next sports that came into existence. Again, these developed as a matter of remaining alive or providing for the family.

Branches were torn from trees and transformed into rough poles which early man used to vault chasms or gorges to find new living areas or better provisions or to escape from an attacking enemy.

Eventually the desire for betterment made itself felt and limber young cavemen challenged each other to vaulting duels. Thus another sport came into being.

The basic benefit from early vaulting was to allow man to cover greater distances horizontally. This fact predominated for many years and in early competition pole vaulting was regarded as a horizontal event rather than one for attaining heights.

History is filled with legends about early day athletics. Teutonic legends tell the story about mighty Siegfried, a champion in sprinting, spear throwing and stone hurling. A burly young man named Cuchullin was the chief Celtic contribution to ancient athletics. This all-around champion starred in the rothcleas, or wheel-feat event, which is thought to be a forerunner of the modern hammer throw. Some historians say that Ireland held the first athletic games about 3000 B. C. A promoter named Luguid the Strong was behind these endeavors which he dedicated to the memory of his foster mother, Queen Tailte.

Latin literature records in the Aeneid of Virgil, the funeral games which included athletic contests. In Sir Walter Scott's "The Lady of the Lake," a Scotsman named Douglas was acclaimed for tossing the caber farther than any other young hero of his day. The caber is a long, heavy beam thrown in early games in the way modern athletes throw the javelin.

Ancient myths of the Egyptians, Hebrews and Arabians give evidence of track and field competition, but certainly the best known early contests were held in Greece.

The Greeks, who admired physical development as much as they did cultural attainment and spiritual ceremonies, combined all three in their early games, some of which go back to 1453 B. C.

At this time the Greeks believed that when anyone died, the spirit of the deceased stayed in the same area where the death occurred. They also felt it was their obligation to entertain these spirits. To do this, they set apart certain days in which to honor their departed friends' spirits.

If the man liked poetry, there would be poetry competition. If he was a music lover, then music would be the feature of the ceremony. If he had had any other likes while alive, these too would be catered to. But an integral part of all these religious rites was athletics.

Archaeologists have uncovered a discus bearing inscriptions of the laws by which the ceremonies would be ruled. The discus, by the way, was the highest symbol of strength. The discus champion was considered the greatest athlete, and all other champions were regarded as his inferiors. Early Greek carvings depict discus throwers in great numbers and the form used then is amazingly similar to the throwing form of today.

Foot racing, along with discus throwing, were the first two events on the program and were followed later by wrestling, jumping and boxing.

The Legend of Pelops goes back to 1307 B. C. and certainly is one of the wildest stories in the history of athletics. It involved sprinting, javelin throwing and chariot racing, offering unusual consequences for the loser.

Pelops was a warrior who lived in the Land Ruled by King Oenomaus, who had a beautiful daughter. Many of the young men in town wanted to marry the daughter. The king said it was all right with him but first they must outwit him. He made a game out of the whole thing. He said the suitors must steal the daughter away from his castle if they wished to marry her. He would try to prevent them.

It sounded easy, but the king had a few tricks up his royal sleeve. When he saw a young man making off with his daughter, he would leap into his chariot and give chase. When he overtook them

A javelin thrower in early competition always had a judge close by who, by pointing with his forked stick, showed the contestant just where to stand.

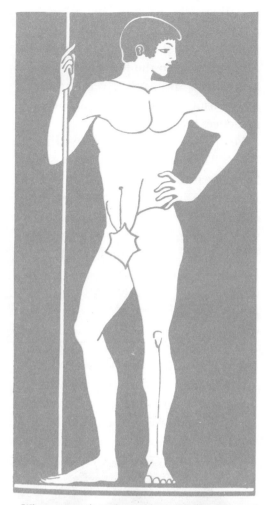

When competing, the track and field athlete of ancient Greece did not bother to put on any clothes.

he'd let fly with a trusty spear and the suitor would bite the dust.

Daring suitors used chariots to try to spirit the daughter away, but the king, who drove an 8-horse chariot, always caught them. By the time Pelops was ready to attempt to steal the daughter away, King Oenomaus had racked up thirteen kills and had frightened (or killed) off most of the eligible bachelors.

But Pelops was resourceful. He bribed the king's mechanic to tinker with the

axle. When Pelops sprinted into the castle and emerged with the daughter, the king gave chase. Just as he aimed his spear the wheel fell off and the king broke his neck as he smashed to the ground.

The king met his untimely end in a village in southwestern Greece called Olympia. Pelops, in honor of the historic occasion, instituted the games and religious rites at that very site.

By 1100 B. C. the Olympics had become established. Only men of high calibre and good family background could enter. They had to take an oath that they were free-born Greeks and never once had broken even the slightest law.

Three of the best in one race were Ulysses, Ajax and Antilochus. As they neared the backstretch, it was Ajax, Ulysses and Antilochus in that order, and it seemed Ajax was well on his way to victory.

Suddenly from the stands out leaped a young woman who proceeded to push and shove Ajax making him trip and stumble. She was Pallas Athene, a friend of Ulysses, who put on a burst of speed and waved politely as he passed the faltering Ajax. Ajax protested to the judges about the girl's actions, but he was overruled for some reason and was awarded second prize — a well-fed bull. Ulysses the winner, was presented with a silver urn.

After this there was a lapse of several hundred years in the games because of the constant intra-mural warfare which continually plagued the Grecians. In 776 B.C. the Olympics were re-born. The authorities decided to have them every four years and they ran consecutively for about 1200 years.

The winner of the first race when the Olympics resumed, was a lad named Coroebus. For his efforts he was presented with an olive wreath crown signifying his supremacy.

However, the olive wreath was only the beginning. Winners were considered minor gods. Their mere appearance on the streets caused great excitement among the young and old alike. Their entire families were honored. Statues were made of the winners and placed among the Olympionicas, an area set apart for perpetuating the victors.

The outstanding athlete was further honored when the next Olympic games were named after him. Upon their triumphant return to their cities, they were accorded parades and festivals. And their entrance was designed for dramatic purposes. Instead of returning through the city gates, the parade marshals simply whacked a hole through the walls, allowing the conquering hero to step through in memorable fashion.

Painters and poets were employed to celebrate his name. They exaggerated quite often, but the occasions gave the writers a chance to outdo each other in praising the athletes. One of the greatest of these was a lyric poet, Pindar, who might be called the Greek Grantland Rice.

Runners always had a coach and official at their back when breaking from the starting position.

An Athenian winner was rewarded with 500 drachma and free food for life in one of the nicer residential districts of Athens, in accordance with the law of Solon.

Since the bounty for winners was so great, several of the competitors were not above hedging a bit. Ancient writings show that long forked rods were kept close by to be used on those who tried to jump the gun.

"Those who start too soon are beaten," said Andeimantus to Themistocles in the council before Salamis.

While most of the winners were treated with overwhelming acclaim, there was one who didn't think his home-folks were receiving him with proper enthusiasm. He was Oebotus of Achaia who was disgruntled because no one raised a statue in his honor.

Miffed because of this oversight, Oebotus hauled off and threw a curse on the town. Sure enough it worked. For seventy-four Olympiads Achaia never had a winner. Finally they got together and raised a statue honoring Oebotus. In the very next Olympic games Sostratas of Achaia won the foot race.

Women were barred from the early Olympics, even as spectators. One near-tragic incident occurred when the mother of Pisidorus, a runner, disguised herself and entered the stadium to watch her son perform. Pisidorus won handily and the shrill, excited feminine shrieks of his mother brought the police on the run. The punishment for a woman to be caught in a stadium at the time was death, with the luckless offender thrown

from a high rock. However because of the gaiety of the occasion she was spared. From then on women were admitted as spectators. And by the 128th Olympic Games women had invaded the winner's circle with Belisiche, a young woman from Macedonia, who came in first in the chariot race.

The athletes were well-trained for the games. There were hot and cold baths in various buildings near the stadium. There were rest rooms with adjoining steam and vapor baths that would be

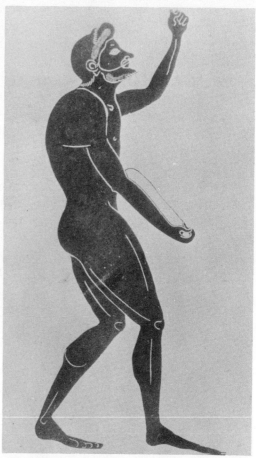

The discus was thrown from a straight position with only a slight turn of the head. The athletes who threw the "diskos," as it was then called, were regarded as national heros.

considered luxurious by today's standards. All competitors had to take a 10-month training program prior to the games. In addition, they underwent an additional 30-day series of workouts under the watchful eyes of Olympic officials. They were placed on a rigid diet. At one early training table the fare called for fresh cheese at all meals with only water to go along with it.

When the Olympics first were begun it was thought that the friendly athletic competition would bring peace to the countless warring tribes within Greece's boundaries. And that was right. For years peace reigned and Greece was able to present a unified fighting force to defend their land against other nations, notably the Persians and the Romans.

As a sidelight, they often held athletic contests while clothed in full suits of armor to develop agility under actual fighting conditions. It was during a Persian invasion in 490 B.C. that one of the most popular Olympic features began.

The Greeks were fighting off the advancing Persians in a city called Marathon while the officials waited back in Athens for word from the front, which they hoped would let them know if the city should be abandoned. The Greeks were more than holding their own and General Miltiades called on Pheidippides, a warrior, to bring the good news back to Athens. Although he had fought through the day, Pheidippides laid down his shield and began the run which measured slightly over 26 miles. Spurred by the good news, he raced toward his goal. His feet cut and bleeding and, near exhaustion, he reached his destination.

"Rejoice; we conquer!" he said. Then he collapsed and died. Every marathon race run from that time on is a tribute to the warrior named Pheidippides.

But there were other enemies who

Full battle equipment adorned the Grecian athletes in order to develop agility under actual fighting conditions.

sought to rule Greece. Among them were the Romans. The Romans came, saw and conquered, but they liked the ideas of the Olympic games. However, under the Romans' direction, they were corrupted and soon the games became a noisy, gay, raucous circus, rather than the honorable religious rites they had been under the Greeks.

The Greeks competed against the Romans and for the first hundred years beat them consistently. Then Rome began developing some fine athletes and became worthy adversaries. Hostility broke out. The Grecians complained that some of the Roman winners were turning the idea of the games into a mercenary venture, charging them with collecting cash for making public appearances. The Romans denied this and there was more bitterness.

At one time, the Romans, angered by charges of the Greeks, stormed into the city and burned buildings, destroying everything they could get their hands on in and around the stadium.

That was too much for Emperor Theodosius I. He ordered the games halted in 394 A.D. In 426 A.D. Theodosius II ordered the razing of the old boundary walls around the Olympic enclosure.

That ended the glorious era of Grecian athletics. For 1500 years there were no Olympics. Finally in 1896, under the guidance of Baron Pierre de Coubertin of Paris, the Olympics were resumed, fittingly enough, in Athens. And, as a further fitting note, the marathon was won by a Greek athlete, S. Loues, the only Grecian winner of the games.

The same idealistic spirit which moved the Greeks to begin their games long ago, inspired the founders of the modern Olympics. It's the spirit which has brought the games to their present exalted status in world-wide athletics.

Champions in full flight. The stride was long and, while running, the palms of the hands were held outward.

Fundamentals
and Techniques

Just about every young person in grade school likes to run. He has foot races in the street, the fields, the school yard, the gymnasium, the playground without worrying about proper fundamentals and techniques. Running while a child of ten or eleven is all fun. It is thrilling to race against others, to outdistance a schoolmate, to get excited about leading a pack to an appointed finish line.

The thrill of the race follows the boy — and some girls — to high school. Here is where he first learns what it means to race in supervised meets. There are instructors, timers, officials and advisors. The youngster now begins to understand that foot-racing is an art, something to be learned through practice and proper conditioning.

The boy who meets with some success in these impromptu events may begin to think seriously of entering varsity competition. If he does, he will learn that there is more to a race than moving arms and legs. Track is one of the difficult sports to master because only the fastest and most dedicated become champions. But track is also a wonderful outlet for a youngster who runs for the sheer delight of expressing his delight at testing his legs and wind against opponent and the clock.

Certainly, not every boy can become a champion. But many can enjoy the thrill of dashing down a dirt lane, leaping over a hurdle or running in the open field, over hills and natural barriers, conserving strength and energy as best he knows how.

There are enough events in track to give every boy an opportunity to compete. The athlete who can best evaluate his own qualifications — helped by a coach's advice — will find track a most stimulating experience.

Sprints

All running events up to 220 yards are called sprints. They are run, for the most part, on straightaway courses. However, the 200-meter race in the Olympic games, and in national Amateur Athletic Union meets, is run around one turn.

A sprinter must have a great deal of natural speed and should also have quick reflexes. His success depends entirely on reacting fast to the starter's gun, hitting top speed in as few strides as possible, then holding that speed until the finish line.

Sprinters come in all shapes and sizes. Champions have included short men like Eddie Tolan and Ira Murchison, who were under five feet, six inches tall; average size men like Jesse Owens and Harold Davis and tall men like Ralph Metcalfe and Andy Stanfield.

The shorter sprinters usually excel at distances from 50 yards through 100 meters (about 110 yards), while the taller ones find their best running range between 100 and 220 yards.

The standard indoor distance for sprinters is 60 yards, while the standard outdoor distances are 100 and 220 yards in American high school and college meets, 100 meters and 200 meters in A.A.U. and Olympic competition.

A good high-school sprinter can run close to 10 seconds for 100 yards and under 23 seconds for 220 yards. Champions run under 10 seconds for the 100 and under 22 seconds for the 220. In college

and A.A.U. meets, championship time is in the 9.3 — 9.6 range for 100 yards, 10.1 — 10.5 for 100 meters and 20.0 — 21.0 for 200 meters and 220 yards.

Though sprinting takes a great deal of natural talent, it also requires a strict training program. A sprinter must learn how to start properly, how to reach top speed in a few strides and how to maintain that speed throughout the race.

In running events, where fatigue is not an element, there are TWO ways to get from one point to another faster than your opponent.

a. One is to move your legs faster.

b. The other, and maybe the SECRET TO SPRINTING, is to have a longer stride and one that carries you low to the ground.

Hal Davis' stride — 9 feet 4 inches.

Bobby Morrow's stride — 9 feet.

There is not much we can do about leg speed except practice. Therefore, we must work on developing the most efficient stride — a long, low one.

Form Exercise. — 1. Walk through this exercise several times. 2. Repeat, bounding forward off toes slowly. 3. Repeat, gradually increasing speed.

a. Lift your knee high.

b. Reach out with your fore leg.

c. Keep high on toes.

d. Reaching out, snap lead leg to the ground.

e. Swing arms parallel to direction of run — not across chest!

f. Arms swing from shoulder, parallel to track.

Reach with lead arm no higher than navel . . . (this keeps you low to ground).

Bring opposite hand back not much farther than your hip.

g. Bound forward, not up. Drive body forward with toes.

h. Maintain good forward lean. This increases stride length.

i. Keep hips forward, back straight. Don't run sitting in a bucket.

Have a straight line from back of head to heel.

A Good Sprinter Will. —

1. Have high knee action.

2. Have good foreleg reach.

3. Run high on toes.

4. Have a good arm action.

5. Bound forward, not up.

6. Maintain good forward lean.

7. Run tall, with back straight.

8. Be relaxed (loose jaw, loose hands).

First Stride in Sprinting. — Careful testing indicates that a sprinter will gain maximum speed off his mark if he cuts his first stride down to a distance of from two feet nine inches to two feet eleven inches.

This stride should be measured from the rear block or starting hole, and not on the starting line.

As the sprinter picks up speed on the next few strides he should lengthen each one by three or four inches until he is running at his normal stride.

This information can be valuable to any runner, Regardless of the distance he runs, a quick start with rapid pick-up is always an advantage.

To improve his ability to get into high gear quickly, the sprinter should check his starting technique carefully during practice, and make certain that his stride length conforms to the figures listed above.

Sprinters must be very careful to warm up properly before running at top speed either in practice or at a meet. There is always the danger of injuring a muscle, particularly during the cool, windy days of early spring. Use of warm-up liniment, under a coach's supervision, can help to prevent these muscle injuries.

A sprinter's training will include work on starts, on striding at three-quarter speed through odd distances like 150 and 300 yards and on sprinting at full speed for 50 to 60 yards from a slow running start. Plenty of calisthenics to limber up the muscles are also included.

Almost every boy starts his track career as a sprinter while still in grammar school. He will soon discover whether he has the talent to continue in these events when he reaches high school. If his speed is just short of the best, he should turn to the hurdles or the middle distances; if he shows little speed at all, he should try longer distances.

The Crouch Start. — At one time, all runners started from a standing position, no matter what the distance of the race. But, in 1888, a Yale University senior introduced the crouch start and, with some improvements on his original style, it has been adopted by every sprinter since that time.

The advantage of the crouch start is that it enables the sprinter to bunch his leg muscles for an explosion which will shoot him rapidly off the marks. It also enables him to launch his body in a half-horizontal position, so that there is less air-resistance to his first few strides.

The major improvement in the crouch start has been the adoption of starting blocks (below and opposite). Before blocks were introduced and legalized, sprinters had to dig their own holes in the track in order to get a proper shove-off place for their feet.

The sprinter on the opposite page is a left-hander and so starts with his left foot back and right foot forward. Right-handers would place the feet in reverse position.

Blocks are set firmly into the ground by spikes at front and rear and are adjustable so that the athlete can place his feet inches apart or separate them by more than a foot. This athlete has elected a placing which leaves his left knee just forward of his right toe and about six inches behind the starting line.

His hands rest just behind the line on the tips of his fingers with the thumbs facing each other. This is the position sprinters take when the starter calls "On Your Marks." Weight should be resting primarily on the left knee at this point.

Once a runner has taken this position, his concentration should be entirely on the commands of the starter. He should look neither to right nor left and his eyes should be fixed on a point on the ground about six feet ahead. If, for any reason, he feels unsettled and unready to start the race, he should call to the starter, who will then tell all of the runners to stand up for awhile.

When the starter is sure that all of the runners are settled on their marks, he will give the next command, "Get Set." There will then be a wait of approximately two seconds for the gun to be shot to start the race. If a runner breaks from the marks before the gun, he is given a warning; if he breaks a second time, he is disqualified.

Beginners often make the mistake of trying to time their start with the gun in order to get a jump on their opponents. This is not only poor sportsmanship, but it is also unwise, as a sprinter who gets into the habit of trying to beat the gun has a hard time breaking it and may never learn to start properly.

Generally the sprinter does not devote enough attention in utilizing his starting blocks to gain momentum quickly. One must practice diligently and be consistent in reminding himself to constantly drive into his blocks, as one of the greatest factors in the sprint start is the amount of momentum that can be obtained.

When the maximum momentum or propulsion from the blocks is obtained by exerting maximum explosive pressure with both feet against the blocks,
times have been improved over the entire distance. Through a series of experiments and tests it has been found that the best position from which to exert foot pressure is a medium foot spread with the hips two to three inches above the shoulders. The knees should be fairly well bent so as to get sufficient drive into the blocks. The start from the blocks is always improved when there is a concentration of hard pressure against the blocks by both feet. This type of a start is usually well adapted to the sprinter with powerfully muscled legs. Associated with the pressure into the blocks should be a definite attempt to lead well with the knees in the first few running strides. Very often sprinters who have increased the strength in the muscles used in the pressure action have improved on their clocking times.

Get Set. — This runner (below) has raised to the "Get Set" position. His weight is now evenly distributed between his arms and legs. He must not lean too heavily on the arms or he will risk falling over as he waits for the gun. There must also be enough weight resting on the rear leg so that he can get a good shove-off.

Notice that the back is perfectly straight, hips at the same level as the head. Some sprinters use an exaggerated uplift of the hips, which is practical if the feet are placed very close together.

The eyes should be fixed on a point on the track three or four feet ahead and the entire concentration of the athlete should be on hearing that gun so that he can react to it immediately.

"Go." — On the break away from the start (above), the arms and legs operate in this order: 1) right arm out and up; 2) left arm back; 3) left leg drives forward about 30 inches; 4) right leg forward about 36 inches. All four of these motions should follow each other within half a second or less.

The motion of both arms and legs should be vigorous, but the backswing of the arms should be halted when the hand has reached the side of the body. Do not bring the body to an erect position too soon; it should be brought up gradually in the first three or four strides.

Shoes worn by a sprinter have the spikes set forward in the sole so that he must run up on his toes. Knees are brought high on every stride and the feet follow a path from the ground up under the hip and then down to the ground again. The arms pump vigorously with the elbow at about a 90-degree angle on both fore-swing and backswing.

Note the tense muscles in the leg. The final drive off the blocks is concentrated in the front leg, in this case the right. The runner, however, must be sure he runs — not "jump" — off the blocks. Otherwise he will lose the smooth motion of arms and legs which brings him to top speed in five or six strides.

Bobby Morrow, one of the finest sprinting champions ever to represent the U.S.A. in the Olympic Games, shows why in this picture as he pours out every ounce of effort to break the tape just a half stride ahead of his competitor from Villanova.

The photograph below shows the start of the 100-meter final of the 1960 Olympics at Rome, Italy.

Armin Hary, Germany, at left, gets his much talked about instinctive start at the gun and is almost a full stride ahead of the other five runners before they even clear the blocks.

All six runners lead with their right foot and explode off the blocks in similar motion although Hary's style appears more polished and personalized from the others. There is little doubt that Hary, who won the race and gold medal, is one of the greatest sprinters of all time.

Dave Sime of the U.S.A., far right, came in second, clocked with Hary at 10.2 seconds.

The sprinter (opposite) takes his second stride out of the blocks. He has come to an erect position a bit too soon, perhaps, but otherwise his form is correct. His right foot will strike the ground with leg vertical from knee down. His body lean is about 20-25 degrees forward and this should be maintained throughout the race.

At the point where the sprinter hits his full running stride (a step of about 5½ to 6½ feet, depending on his height), he settles into the form he will hold until the finish line. His legs should drive as straight as the pistons of a machine — there should be no wavering to right or left, as in the start on page 33. He should run a perfectly straight course to the finish line, as crossing over into another runner's lane means disqualification.

No change in running style should be made in the ten yards which precede the finish. Nor should a runner change stride when he sees another athlete in front of him. He would only fall further behind if he lost his form.

The sprinter should run right through the finish line to a point at least three yards beyond, then slow down gradually. In an extremely close finish, he may dip his chest slightly into the tape, but no lunge or leap at the string will get him there any faster.

Morrow (below) wins a 220-yard dash. He strides along formfully, showing no strain, while the runner at left displays his tenseness in his facial expression. In the center, hurdle champion Glenn Davis, in an effort to catch the leaders, is leaning too far back with his body.

Another runner (right) shows proper form at the finish line of the 220. There is no strain in either arms or legs as he floats along and his stride is slightly longer than would be practical in a shorter race.

This style of running is called "floating" and it enables a sprinter to coast along through the middle 100-120 yards of a 220 without the strain of hard sprinting. It can only be mastered after a great deal of training, including work at distances from 300 to 440 yards.

35

On these pages you find a sequence of photos showing the unusual starting style of one of the world's great sprinters, Bobby Morrow, 1956 Olympic champion at both 100 and 200 meters.

Unlike most sprinters, Morrow places his feet almost evenly on the starting blocks, the right perhaps a bit ahead of the left. (Photo below left.) This foot position leaves his left knee much closer to the ground than is normal.

Raising to the set position, below center, Morrow's legs are almost parallel to each other. His position is like that of a football lineman raising himself for a charge. It would be impossible to tell which leg is going to take the first step.

Below, Morrow drives out with his right leg, the one which was slightly advanced in his set position. He swings his arms violently as if to make up for any lack of drive from his legs.

The advantage in Morrow's style is shown in the picture below left. Though he has completed only the first step from the blocks, he is already in an almost upright position, and, in the next photo, he has come completely erect by his third step.

This quick move to vertical running form has enabled Morrow to hit full speed earlier than his rivals in most of his races. He may lose a little in the first few steps, but, by not spending as much time shifting into top gear, he quickly catches up and passes his foes.

A sprinter starts somewhat like an automobile, moving from high-pressure low gear, through second gear and into high speed top gear. Morrow makes a quicker shift than his rivals, just as does fluid drive in a car.

A head-on view (left) of a sprinter showing the driving form used in a shorter dash. Note that the right foot is up under the hip as the knee is lifted. His left arm is lifted with his right knee and the right arm swings back until the hand is even with the side.

A sprinter must not take a fully extended forward stride with his leg or he would waste too much time getting it back into position for the next step. As the foot touches the ground, the weight of the body should be centered directly over it or slightly ahead of it.

The sprinter (below) hits the finish line. His head motion is slightly exaggerated as he flings it back with his arms in order to bring the chest forward slightly from the waist so that the chest hits the tape.

Since they are so short, many sprint races produce some close finishes, sometimes so close that the judges have a difficult time deciding who won. It is important that a sprinter know the rules by which a finish is judged so that he will not lose the race by a mistake at the tape.

It is the runner who hits the tape first with some part of his body between waist and upper chest who wins the race. The head does not count, nor do the arms or legs. Should a runner fall, he is judged to have finished the race when his body from head to hips has slid over the line.

Who won the race? (opposite page) The judges said it was the man at right, who is breaking the tape with his head. But the rules would say that it was the man at left who leans into the tape with his chest.

Controversial sprint decisions form one of the more exciting pages in track and field history. The best rule is always to try to finish like the runner at left, for he is the one who normally would get the judges' nod.

Another close finish (below) which shows what perfect form can do for a runner. Look first at the runners' feet and notice that the man at the extreme right clearly has his foot ahead of his rivals, in fact over the finish line.

But then look at the chests of the other athletes and you will see that he is being beaten to the tape by the two men at left. The best finishing form is displayed by the runner at left, who won the race.

The finish (opposite page, above) of a 100-meter dash. The winner, far right, shows perfect running form as he strides into the tape. Notice how some of the athletes in the rear have lost their form. The man third from left is driving his right leg too far forward and the left one has come back so far that the foot is higher than the hip.

The runner at the far left is making the same error. All six runners are at approximately the same point of their stride, but the back foot of the leader is anywhere from one to two feet lower than that of his rivals and will have that much less distance to travel on his next stride into the tape.

In a close finish (right) in the 60 yard dash Joe Cianciabella of Manhattan shows fine finishing form while breasting the tape a split second before Glenn Davis of Army. The extra effort shown here not only earned a victory for the winner of this race, he also tied the intercollegiate AAAA record which had been set nine years before.

The number of close finishes has resulted in the introduction of photo-timing devices in many major meets. They are only used when the judges disagree. There also have been experiments with artificial starting devices which would prevent athletes from "jumping" the gun.

Running

In addition to the sprints, the running events also include the middle distance races (440 yards through one mile) and the long distance races (two miles and more).

High-school athletes are restricted to the middle distances, except in cross-country when they may run 1.8 or two and a half miles. The standard outdoor distances for high-school races are 440 yards, 880 yards and one mile. Indoor meets often substitute the 300 or 600-yard run for the 440 and the 1000-yard run for the 880.

A standard outdoor track is oval-shaped and measures 440 yards for one lap. Indoor tracks have no standard size, as they must fit the arena in which they are located. The most common sizes, however, are 10 laps to a mile (176 yards) and 8 laps to a mile (220 yards).

Outdoor tracks are composed of hard clay or cinders and runners use shoes with six half-inch spikes set in the sole. Indoor tracks are of hardwood and runners may use either short spikes or none at all.

Though it is the most natural of all sports, running requires a great deal of practice and conditioning. Champions stay in training the year-round, increasing their work during the competitive season, slacking off a little in the off-season.

Here is the typical training schedule of a high school middle-distance runner:

Cross-country work, September-December; indoor running or gymnastic work, December-early March; outdoor running, early April-mid-June.

This schedule will vary according to where the athlete lives. In warm climates, indoor training can be omitted and outdoor work begun as early as February. As a competitive sport, indoor track is popular only in the colder regions of the United States, such as the Northeast and Middle West.

Champion runners come in every size and shape, but have one thing in common: there is no extra weight on their frame. In fact, a runner in training will normally be 10-15 pounds lighter than another boy of the same general size and build. Coaches keep a careful watch on a runner's weight during the season, to be sure it does not drop too low. If this does happen, a short rest from training will usually bring back the lost weight.

A middle-distance runner must keep a careful watch on his diet, avoiding fatty foods, starches and fried dishes. On the days of the meets, he should eat a substantial, energy-producing meal five or six hours before he runs, then eat very lightly an hour or so prior to the race.

Some runners are successful at a wide range of distances, but, more often, a runner will find that he excels at one particular event, such as the 880, but only has fair success at other races of comparable distance, such as the 440 and mile.

All middle-distance runners must have a fair amount of speed, but, the longer the race, the less speed and the more endurance they require. Sprinters, for in-

43

stance, can usually be made into good 440-yard men, but would not have the endurance to run a mile.

Four qualities are found in most middle distance champions: 1. speed, 2. endurance, 3. good running form, 4. judgment of pace and racing tactics.

Speed is a natural gift which can be improved only slightly by training. Endurance also is born into an athlete, but this can be improved considerably through training. Running form and race sense are the product of good coaching.

A runner's form will depend on the distance of the race, but, in all cases, it should omit any unnecessary movements of body, arms and legs. Muscles should be kept relaxed except when the athlete is sprinting at the start or finish of the race or when trying to pass a runner.

Generally speaking, the longer the race is, the lower the knee is lifted on each stride. The arms are also held lower in long-distance races and the athlete no longer runs high on his toes as in the sprints. In middle distance races, he will strike the ground on the ball of his foot, in long distance races with both heel and sole.

Since an athlete cannot run the entire distance of even a 440-yard race at top speed, he must pace himself so that he will stay with the leaders and still have enough strength for a sprint (kick) at the finish. Most major middle distance races are won in the last 100 yards.

The best plan is for the runner to break fast from the start, settle into a position where he can run freely and then start his kick when he feels able to sprint all the way to the tape.

Some runners prefer to go right into the lead and stay there. Others like to settle just behind the leader. In the latter case, the runner should take a position off the outside right shoulder of the leader, prevent anyone moving up on his own right side and boxing him in.

Pacing in a quarter-mile is somewhat like that in a 220. The athletes run hard for the first 100 yards, go into a fast float for the next 220 yards, then drive hard for the tape. In the 880 or mile, an athlete can learn, through practice, to run each lap of the race to an exact timetable.

A runner should try to avoid passing other athletes, or being passed himself, too often during a race. Each pass requires extra effort and takes away some of the speed from the final kick. A good rule is to decide before the race in what position you will run, then stay there until ready to make your final move.

At right (opposite), is the usual position on the starting line for races of 880 yards. Many 880 men use starting blocks because of the added momentum it gives them at the start of the race and the using up of nervous energy. (Quarter-milers normally start from the sprint start.) For longer races a runner stands with one foot up to the line, the other slightly behind. He is leaning forward, but rests enough weight on the back leg to get a good shove-off when the gun fires.

Two of the great middle-distance stars, Herb Elliott and Merv Lincoln, of Australia (opposite) are shown on their way to breaking four minutes for the mile. They are sprinting for the tape, using a vigorous arm movement and bringing the knee high.

The four-minute mile was one of the great achievements of track and field history. High-school athletes, however, are satisfied to break 4:30 for the mile, while their targets in the 440 and 880 are, respectively, 50 seconds flat and two minutes flat.

Above, the runner is in full 440-yard stride. His left leg drives up only a little lower than in a sprint, but the arms swing lower and more loosely. The body lean is only about 15 degrees. Head is carried high so that there is no danger of a bent neck cutting off the normal flow of air to the lungs.

The runner (right) completes his forward stride with the left leg. The foot comes a little forward of the knee and will strike on the ball of the foot. The right leg is allowed to come up easily behind the body before it is brought forward.

46

The pictures above and below are shots of the 800 meters final at the Olympic Games of 1960 in Rome, Italy.

Heading into the homestretch Christian Waelge of Switzerland was setting the pace with Roger Moens of Belgium, world record holder and favored to win the race, in second place. Peter Snell, a powerfully built New Zealander, was running a close third. As the pack spread out on the final burst for the tape, it was Snell beating Moens by a split stride and one of the most surprising upsets of the Games. Snell, just 21 years of age, related after his victory that he had been sent to the Games merely for the experience. However, after four fast runs in three days against the stiffest competition possible, his confidence had mounted so high that it was his competitors and the fans who were more surprised than he at his victory.

One of the great middle-distance runners of all time, 1956 Olympic 800-meter champion Tom Courtney (above), leads the field in his semi-final. This field is more closely bunched with six runners separated by less than five yards.

All six runners are now sprinting for the tape, knees driving high and arms swinging upward. But, while Courtney moves smoothly, with no strain apparent in legs, body or facial expression, the four runners to the rear are evidently struggling to keep up. By setting a slow pace over the first 400 meters, Courtney was able to save his greater speed for this final stage of the race.

Notice that the runners third from right and far right are bringing their feet up under their hips, just as they would in a sprint. All runners, no matter what their favorite distance, must work on sprinting style, so that they can keep their form in the dash for the tape, as loss of form can cause loss of time.

Outdoor meets are held in almost any kind of weather and a runner must be prepared to compete under such conditions as shown above. When running on a muddy, or water-covered track, an athlete must slow down his normal pace, as each stride will take an extra amount of energy. He should also avoid running directly behind another athlete, as he would soon be covered with mud from the backswing of the leader's legs.

The three athletes above are moving along during a mile run. Two are holding their position with normal strides, but the runner on the left is sprinting to get into the lead. His knees drive high-

er, he is landing more on the toe of his foot and his body lead is more pronounced.

Notice the strides on the runners at far right and on the left. The leader's left leg hits the ground with knee slightly bent. The other man's left leg hits the ground extended straight from hip to toe. The first stride is known as the "European," the second as the "American." The European stride allows a higher back kick of the leg, the American more of a forward kick.

A view of a 600-yard run at Madison Square Garden with 1956 Olympic 400-meter champion Charles Jenkins in the

lead (above). Notice the way the runners lean in, dropping their left shoulder, as they take the turn. Unless a runner does this, the force which he builds up on the straightaway will carry him high on the narrow, banked turns and force him to lose form and speed, as well as run a few extra yards.

Indoor running requires a great deal more experience in tactics than outdoor running. The crowded conditions on the narrow tracks, the many turns, the difficulty in passing another runner enable veteran athletes to hold their own even against faster, stronger youngsters.

51

Little did these six starters realize when they rose from their starting positions that they were about to be a part of the most historic race in all of racing. This is how it was in Oxford, England, on May 6, 1954 when Roger Bannister began his assault on foot-racing's most unbreakable barrier — the four-minute mile.

Bannister, third from left, had ideal conditions for his attempt. The weather was cool and brisk and the competition was strong enough to spur him on to the greatest race of his life.

Bannister broke easily and in good po-sition. He probably received some advantage by being placed in the middle of the field and drove clear of any swinging arms or hips.

In the sequence on the opposite page Bannister shows his long, powerful stride midway through the race. The "kick" from his left leg is made after it has been raised to a 90-degree angle. As he rises on his right instep, his left leg goes forward in a long, powerful motion and his hands and arms are carried above his hips. This was the stride Roger used when he was within the last fifty yards of the tape.

During the first quarter-mile Bannister seemed unconcerned, unhurried. He kept to his pre-race plan of permitting a pace-setter to take over and as the field rounded the first turn he had already moved over to the inside lane, in perfect position to assume the lead.

Running almost in identical fashion are Bannister and the pace-setter. They seem to be moving at the same pace, the same stride. Their right forearms are in similar position and the leader's left hand is only a shade lower than Bannister's. Their left legs are lifted at exactly the same time and seem to be held in the same position.

Bannister was all alone as he came flying down the stretch, moving strongly and surely away from the field. He held his final ounces of energy for his assault on the clock — no longer was there any doubt about finishing first. As he came to the tape (opposite), his breathing was labored and he kept his mouth open, inhaling through both his nose and mouth to get a sufficient amount of air.

The Finish. — The finish of a middle-distance race is just as important as the finish of a sprint. The athlete must carry his kick right through the tape and, if it is a close finish, use a dip of the body to break the string first.

Since 440 and 880-yard runners are often required to run heats before the final of their races, they must be able to qualify in these heats without expending all of the energy needed for the final. However, they should not make the common mistake of slowing up as they near the finish in a qualifying position, then seeing another runner pass them in the last few strides. It is a better idea to hold back during the major portion of the race, allowing someone else to set the pace, then come through with a fast finish.

Below is the finish of the race pictured on page 49, the 1956 Olympic 800-meter semi-final, with Courtney breaking the tape (below). The runners are even more bunched now than they were coming off the last turn. At right is the photo-timing device which will be used to settle any disputes of the judges about the order of finish. It takes a picture of each man as he hits the finish line on a revolving negative and thus shows the athletes in their order of passing the tape.

At right is the great Ron Delaney of Ireland setting an indoor world's record of 4:02.5 for the mile at Madison Square Garden. Running with a style all his own, Delaney won the 1956 Olympic 1500-meter title and campaigned successfully at distances from 440 yards through five miles.

As he strides through the tape, Delaney is the picture of relaxation even

over and under his specialty to build up speed and endurance. He also works on pace work, doing so many laps at a time set by his coach.

Distance runners have no specialty, but compete in two classes: track runners, from two through six miles; road runners, from 10 miles through the marathon distance of 26 plus miles. Some distance men try both types of running.

Training twice a day, morning and evening to avoid midday heat, a distance runner will do most of his work on the grass, using the track only occasionally for pacing.

Distance training methods vary, but the most effective seems to be the Swedish system of "Fartlek" (Speed-play). It consists of long runs on the grass, alternating fast and slow paces. It is designed to build endurance, increase speed for

after his fast, hard race. His arms swing easily at his sides and his angular legs show nothing but bone and muscle.

Right is the finish of a world's record 400-meter race, won by Grover Klemmer in 46.0, in 1947. This was the first race in which six runners broke 47.0 for the distance. Notice how all of the runners are driving for the finish line in perfect form, bodies erect, knees lifted high and no sign of strain in their muscles or features.

Distance Running. — The training for distance races — two miles and over — differs from that for the middle distances in many ways. A middle distance runner trains chiefly on the track at distances

the finishing kick and also to help the athlete escape the monotony of long runs at a steady, boring pace.

The stride of a distance runner is a shortened version of the European stride shown on page 50. The athlete allows his body to carry his legs along, feet rising high behind the body, then dropping forward to hit the track. There is almost no knee-lift, except in the sprint for the tape. The foot strikes on heel and sole, so a distance runner wears heels on his track shoes.

Women in Running. — Most running for women is at sprint distances from 50 through 220 yards, but some competition is also held at 440 yards, 880 yards and a mile, as well as the metric equivalents of 400 meters, 800 meters and 1500 meters.

Above is a women's 800-meter race. Notice that the leader, second from left, and several of the other girls as well, are planting their full foot on the ground unable to stay up on their toes. Track and field is a healthy sport for girls, but one that has never become too popular in the United States. It enjoys great success in Eastern European countries, as well as in England and Australia.

Marjorie Jackson (above) of Australia wins the 100 meters at the 1952 Olympic games. The girls exhibit good sprinting form with knees driving high and body leaning forward. Their speed is naturally not equal to that of men, their best times for the 100 yards or 100 meters being about a second slower. Nor do they have anywhere near the endurance for the longer races, with 60 seconds for the 440, 2:20 for the 880 and 5:15 for the mile being considered good times.

Steeplechase

The steeplechase is one of the rarest events in American track and field meets. It is usually run only in district and national A.A.U. championships, or in the Olympic tryouts.

Distance for the Olympic steeplechase event is 3,000 meters, but races are also run at two miles in the United States. On each lap, competitors must clear five three-foot high hurdles, one a water jump (see opposite page).

Tall distance runners with strong springy legs usually make the best steeplechasers. Very often, athletes who are not quite of championship class in flat, long races turn to this event. This is particularly true in the United States.

The hurdles used in steeplechase events have broad tops which allow an athlete to step on them and shove off if he is too tired to hurdle them cleanly. A runner is even allowed to use his hands to vault over the hurdles, but is disqualified if he should run around them.

A special technique is used in taking the water jump. The runner leaps to the top of the hurdle with his lead off foot, then shoves off hard and tries to land in the far end of the twelve-foot wide pool. The lead runner in the picture at left has successfully taken the jump in this manner, the second man is floundering in deep water, and the third, having missed his footing on top of the hurdle, is about to fall on his face.

Steeplechasers must develop the ability to take the "dry" hurdles leading with either right or left leg as they cannot time their steps as do hurdlers in shorter races. In practice, they set up hurdles at regular intervals around the track, then run several laps, clearing the hurdles as they come to them.

Otherwise, training for the steeplechase is the same as for any other distance race. The stride used is also the same, except in the steps immediately before each hurdle, when it is lengthened a bit.

Because of the obstacles on the course, strategy in a steeplechase race will vary slightly from that in other distance races. Runners must be very careful not to be caught in any boxes which would interfere with their free approach to a hurdle. One fall will usually eliminate them from contention.

A boy who has had some success as a cross-country runner or a miler in high school and who also shows talent in jumping events can often become a fine steeplechaser. But the limited competition in the event makes it impossible to concentrate only on this race and so he must also run flat distance races to keep a sharp competitive edge.

Steeplechasing is much more popular in Europe than in the United States and the event is included in almost every major track and field meet held on that continent.

The picture below was taken at an international meet held in the Berlin stadium. Notice that the water jump is not located on the running track itself, but off to one side.

Of the three competitors going over the water jump, two are using the step-off method, the other is clearing in regular hurdle fashion.

The runner at the left has just placed his right foot on the hurdles and his left arm is swung high to help carry his left leg over the hurdle. He does not bend the left leg as would a high or low hurdler, but uses the push off with his right leg to get it over the hurdle cleanly.

The runner at the right is ready to shove off. He has brought his body up high with the force of his shove and the left leg has cleared easily. Both arms are in front of his body to help maintain balance.

Notice that both runners in the water also have their arms forward as they struggle to regain balance, while the leading runner at right has already settled back into normal stride.

The picture (opposite) was taken at the 1956 Olympic Games at Melbourne and the competitor caught in mid-air over the water jump. Chris Brasher of England, was the eventual winner.

Here we see five runners, reading from right to left, in various stages of the correct form at the water jump.

The competitor at right brings his right knee high and swings his left arm up as he takes off.

The next runner is about to land on the hurdle with his right foot as the left leg follows with knee bent.

Brasher has already shoved off after landing on the hurdle with his left foot. His right leg reaches forward and he keeps his eyes downward to help insure a safe landing.

The competitor at the far left is ready to execute a perfect landing near the end of the pool, eyes still cast downward until his foot hits the water and right leg ready for the next stride onto land.

The runner in the foreground has made his landing and his right leg reaches forward to stride out of the pool.

Notice that most of the runners are tall and lean with well-defined leg muscles, well able to take the shock of more than thirty landings during the race.

Low Hurdles

The low hurdles are run at the 200-meter or 220-yard distance in college and A.A.U. meets, but, in high school, the distance is only 180 yards. In all cases, the hurdles are separated by 20 yards and the distance from the starting line to the first hurdle, and from the final hurdle to the finish, is also 20 yards.

An athlete who runs the low hurdles need not be as tall, nor as agile as a high hurdler. Most high hurdlers also run the lows, and sprinters also have great success in this event.

The low hurdles are seldom run outside of the United States. Athletes of other nations concentrate on the 400-meter medium hurdles, which are included in the Olympic program. The low hurdles were dropped from the Olympics years ago.

There are 10 hurdles in the 220-yard or 200-meter hurdles, but only eight hurdles in the 180-yard event. Good time for the 180-yard distance is 21 seconds, while champions run it under 20 seconds. For the 220-yard distance, 25 seconds is a good time, while the top runners go below 23 seconds.

The low hurdles are often run around a turn, just as are the 220-yard or 200-meter dashes. In this case, time will be slowed down by almost half a second as the hurdlers have a great deal of trouble adjusting their steps between hurdles.

A low hurdler normally takes ten steps to the first hurdle and seven steps between hurdles (this does not include the step over the hurdle itself).

The most difficult problem in the low hurdles is for the athlete to keep his legs and body low enough so he just clears the barrier. High hurdlers, in particular, tend to soar too high over the lower barriers and waste extra seconds in the air. Sprinters, unused to the form of hurdling, also jump higher than necessary, just to be sure they don't hit a barrier.

A boy who tries out for the low hurdles usually will also participate in other events. His training time, therefore, is divided between his various events and he may not spend enough time on the low hurdles as a result.

If he is a high hurdler, he will practice that event and hope that his form there will be suitable for the low barriers as well. If he is a sprinter, he will work on his speed and starts and count on them to overcome any faults in style.

One way to avoid this neglect of the low hurdles is to set a certain amount of practice time each week to work exclusively on form over the two-foot, six-inch barriers. Pick a day when the rest of the training schedule is light.

Take two or three hurdles, set them twenty yards apart and go over this shortened course one time after another, until the rhythm of the steps is perfect and the legs and body skim the hurdle with scarcely an inch or two of clearance.

The body lean of a low hurdler is much less than in the high hurdles. Some runners merely dip their upper body forward for an instant at the point of clearance. The arms follow the natural motion of sprinting, though the trailing arm may be held out from the side a little to help maintain proper balance.

A low hurdler must pace himself through the race, just as does a 220-yard runner. He cannot drive all the way or his leg muscles might tighten and make it impossible for him to maintain his stride over the last few hurdles. A good system is to drive hard for the first two hurdles, relax slightly into a floating stride over the next four, then drive again over the last four.

A runner is shown as he approaches the first hurdle (opposite). His running form is that of a sprinter, knees driving high and arms swinging vigorously. But his body is more erect and each stride is measured so that he will arrive at the barrier in position for a fast clearance.

Low hurdlers, like high hurdlers and sprinters, often have to run heats and semi-finals in championship meets. Unlike middle-distance runners, they have no chance to take it easy in the early stages of a race, so, if they are to save a little extra strength for the finals, they must ease up when they are sure of a qualifying berth.

No hurdler should ever relax in a heat until he has cleared the last barrier. He may then take a quick look to see that no one is in position to beat him out for a spot in the finals, then slow down a bit if he wishes.

Low hurdle races are sometimes run in indoor meets at the 60 and 70-yard distances. In this case, the hurdles are

placed 10 yards apart with 15 yards to the first hurdle. The runners use the same step-count in these races as they would for the high hurdles.

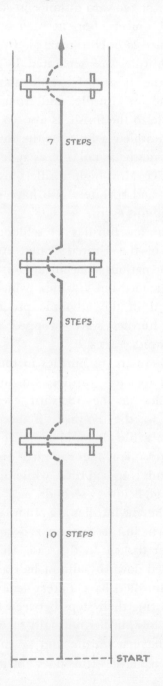

In the first picture of this sequence, left, the tremendous forward drive of the runner is very apparent. This forward rush of the body will give him effortless lift over the hurdle.

The knee lift of the lead leg is somewhat more severe than just a normal stride.

In addition to being an exciting event to compete in, the low hurdles also provide fine training for other events. Some coaches insist that their young sprinters and quarter-milers run the low hurdles in freshman and sophomore years.

The necessity to stretch out the stride in the low hurdles in order to get the proper step-count between hurdles forces the runner to use a more relaxed style and often helps to improve his speed.

Upper body leans forward into the driving stride.

Rear leg hesitates slightly, then pumped to the outside to about h height with knee bent and foot trailin instep parallel to ground.

Right

Wrong

Precise details in form is more desirable in the high hurdles than the low hurdles. In the lows the hurdler should run over the hurdles with a nearly unbroken rhythm at top running speed and fine details of form interfere with smooth forward drive.

The very best low hurdle stylists almost seem to run over the barrier as if it wasn't there at all. Thus an athlete who can barely run under 21 seconds for 220 yards, like Elias Gilbert, is able to set a world's low hurdle record in 22.1. This means that each clearance of a hurdle added little more than a tenth of a second to his normal time for the distance.

The rear leg comes through with a late burst of action.

Contact after clearing hurdle is made on ball of foot of lead leg as following leg, knee still high, levels off and stretches out for full power stride.

As lead foot pushes off body straightens again to a normal erect running position.

The runner lands on the other side of the hurdle (opposite), his left foot hitting on the toe and the right leg swinging forward for the next stride. His arms are now in their normal sprinting position (compare their position with the picture on page 67 of the same boy approaching the first hurdle).

The hurdler has landed only about three or four feet away from the barrier, rather than the five feet or so which is customary in a high hurdle race. His weight is centered a little forward of the landing foot and he is ready to drive on to the next barrier.

A world's record in the 400-meter hurdles is being set by Glenn Davis (above, left), in the 1956 American Olympic trials. His rival, matching him stride for stride, is Eddie Southern, then only 18 years old. Night meets such as this one are quite popular in many parts of the world, as they allow more spectators to watch the athletes and take the athletes away from the hot summer sun.

A boy who has had any success in the low hurdles in high school and who has also shown ability at the quarter-mile, should begin work on the 400-meter hurdles as soon as he reaches college. He may not get many opportunities to run this race, but persistence could pay off handsomely in an Olympic year.

On these pages are three views of the greatest woman athlete of all time, Mildred (Babe) Didrikson, setting a world's record in the trials and then winning the final of the 80-meter hurdles for women at the 1932 Olympic games.

In the 80-meter hurdles, the eight barriers are placed eight meters (about nine yards) apart, with 12 meters to the first hurdle and 12 meters from the last hurdle to the finish line.

The Babe shows her great sprinting form (below) as she drives to a world's record in her heat. Contrast her vigorous leg and arm movements with those of her rivals.

Babe clears a hurdle in the final (left), with her left foot practically skimming the top. Just for fun, in practice, Babe would put coins on top of the hurdle and regularly knock them off without hitting the wood.

At right, Babe wins the final, barely hitting the tape ahead of her teammate, Evelyn Hall.

Here are four women hurdlers competing at a meet in London (below). The form of three of them is excellent, but the girl at left has her knee bent far too much as she lifts her lead foot to the hurdle.

Hurdle Relay. — Hurdlers also have their relay race, just as runners on the flat do, but it is run much differently. It would be impossible, because of the measured steps needed in a hurdle race, to set the barriers around the track and have the four men pass a baton.

Instead, a hurdle relay is run as a shuttle, back and forth, usually on the grass field inside the oval of the track. Enough hurdles are set up so that each team has two flights all to itself.

The first man runs down over one flight, touches off his teammate, who then runs back on the other flight. This gives officials a chance to pick up any hurdles which are knocked down before they will be needed again. Should any runner start moving before touched by his teammate, or should any member of a team violate the rules of hurdling, the team is disqualified.

These shuttle relays may be run with either high or low hurdles. But if the low hurdles are used, only five rows are set up at the usual intervals. Shuttle hurdle relays give a coach a chance to test his younger boys in competition.

One of the qualities of a hurdler which has not yet been mentioned is the need for courage. Before a boy becomes a good hurdler, and even after that happens, he will take his full share of spills. He will also bang knees, shins and feet against the hurdles and have a good assortment of bruises to show for it.

The hurdle itself therefore presents a challenge to every runner. He must conquer it first before he can conquer his rivals in a race. His form must be letter perfect and he must be calm enough to control every stride even in the heat of competition. Only when the final barrier has been safely passed are hurdle rivals on a man-to-man basis in the sprint for the tape.

If a hurdler has no chance to compete during the winter months, he may still get valuable practice setting up one or two hurdles in a gymnasium and working on form. Winter is a good time to start beginners in this event by setting gymnastic horses at the proper hurdle height, then having the boys slide over them with sweat clothes on to protect the legs from friction burns.

Lee Calhoun wins the high hurdles at the Olympic
Trials tying the American record of 13.4 seconds.
Willie May (right) was a close second with a time
of 13.5.

High Hurdles

The speed of a sprinter, the spring of a high jumper and the endurance of a quarter-miler are among the qualities of a champion hurdler.

Hurdle races are run at various distances and with barriers of different height. High hurdles are 3 feet, 6 inches high; medium hurdles stand 3 feet high and low hurdles are 2 feet, 6 inches high. However, in high school, the high hurdles are only 3 feet, 3 inches high.

The regular outdoor distance for a high hurdle race is 120 yards, while indoor races are usually run at 60 yards. The medium hurdles are run at 400 meters or 440 yards, while the low hurdles are run at 180 yards in high school, at 200 meters or 220 yards in college or A.A.U. meets.

Hurdlers are normally tall, slim boys, who also compete in such events as the sprints, 440, broad jump or high jump. They should have almost as much speed as a champion sprinter and enough spring to become a 20-foot broad jumper or 5-foot-10 high jumper with sufficient practice in those events.

Because of the difference in the height of the barriers, high school and college runners do about the same time for the high hurdles. For the 120-yard distance, a time under 16 seconds is fair, one under 15 seconds is good and anything under 14 seconds is in the championship class.

Since the hurdler uses the start and the stride of a sprinter when not actually clearing the barriers, he must practice starts and sprint form as part of his training. But he must also spend a lot of time on his hurdling form, on exercises to loosen his body muscles and on perfecting his steps between the hurdles.

There are 10 hurdles in a 120-yard event, set as follows: 15 yards to the first hurdle, 10 yards between each of the hurdles and 15 yards from the last hurdle to the finish line. It takes a runner seven or eight steps to get to the first hurdle and, not counting the hurdle step itself, he must take just three steps between each hurdle.

The proper position of the legs in clearing a hurdle is as follows:

Front leg is extended forward with knee almost straight. The rear leg is bent to the outside as it leaves the ground and crosses the hurdle in a level position parallel with the top of the barrier. The knee of this leg is bent so that the heel touches the back of the thigh.

After the front leg crosses the hurdle, it must snap down sharply so that the runner does not "sail" over the barrier and waste valuable time. He must work on his form until he can practically knock a coin off the top of the hurdle without actually touching the barrier itself.

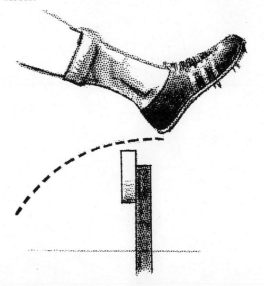

As the hurdler (left) takes off, his left foot stretches out toward the hurdle, with the right arm also pointing straight ahead. The rear leg bends sidewise as it leaves the ground, with the heel beginning to come forward to meet the thigh.

This sequence of high hurdle pictures show excellent and graceful form. They present to you the opportunity to follow through all the important individual actions of body, legs and arms that combine to give a hurdler fine coordination, which is very necessary to accomplish sharp timing and top hurdling form.

A hurdler may lead with whichever leg feels most natural to him. Depending on which leg he leads with, and how many steps (seven or eight) it takes him to the first hurdle, he will have to adjust his feet properly in the crouch start. Often, a boy who normally would start with right foot back must put the left foot back instead so that he will arrive at the barrier in proper position.

The position of the left arm in crossing the barrier is up to the individual runner. Some hold it forward, some at the side and some to the rear as subsequent illustrations will show.

As he starts over the barrier (below), the hurdler just clears it with the heel of the left foot. The right leg is now decidedly bent at the knee, which still must be brought out sidewise.

The body lean is well forward. This is extremely important, for, when the hurdler hits on the other side of the barrier his body weight must be over or even a little ahead of his lead leg so that he can go right into sprinting form. A backward lean will slow him down and make fast time less possible.

The farther forward you can accomplish body lean over the hurdle and retain good balance, the more drive you can get into your first stride toward the next hurdle.

As he lands on the other side of the hurdles, the athlete swings his right leg forward, bringing the knee and lower leg back to normal position for the next stride. His weight is located over his left leg and he has the balance necessary to take a firm, fast stride with the right.

Strong ankles are necessary for the hurdler to absorb the shock of each landing without losing his balance. Notice that in all three pictures the athlete kept his eyes looking squarely ahead, neither looking down, nor to right or left. A hurdler must run his race as if there were no other runners in it, for should he see someone gaining on him to right or left, he would be tempted to start sprinting harder, lose his timing and miss a step.

The runner on left (below) has already dropped his front foot, but still has less of a knee bend than his rival. His left leg sticks out at 90 degrees from his hip and is parallel to the top of the barrier as it goes over. He keeps his right arm at his side and uses only a slight body lean.

The leader, at right, swings his left arm back as he lands, with his left leg driving straight forward for the next step.

Notice that neither runner is paying any attention to his rival. Both are concentrating on their chief job, which is to clear the hurdles.

An athlete is allowed to knock down as many of the barriers as he wishes during a race without being disqualified. But he will be disqualified should he run around a hurdle, or allow any part of his trailing leg to come around the side of the hurdle instead of going over it.

Each hurdler must develop his own style of carrying his arms as he clears the barriers. Some throw both arms forward; others extend one arm forward and the other back; still others swing one arm out to the side. Whichever style gives you the best balance while not cutting down your speed is best for you.

Above are several different arm styles. From left, the first two hurdlers throw left arm forward pointing down so that it is almost parallel to the leading right leg. The right arm, meanwhile, is held just about at the side, though the hurdler at extreme left sticks it out farther to the side than the other man. The hurdler second from right leads with his left leg, so it is his right arm which is held forward, slightly to the side, while the left arm (only hand visible) is held tightly to his side. The man at far right also leads with his left leg, but he swings his right arm high in the air to one side and extends his left arm forward.

Opposite, below, more arm styles can be seen. The salute-like extension of the lead arm, which aids balance but can hurt speed, is used by the hurdler at left and the man third from left. The man between them swings his left arm well forward and the right arm back. The one second from right holds his right arm off to the side, almost as a football player will when running with the ball to ward off a tackler.

Notice that Harrison Dillard, second from the right, already has a clear edge on the field though this is only the first hurdle in the race. Many races are won in the sprint for the first barrier. The runner who gets there first will have no distractions as he goes over the barrier; men behind him may misjudge their timing as they try to catch up.

Above, a hurdler is seen clearing the last barrier in an indoor event. Here, the dash for the first hurdle is all-important, as the race will be no more than sixty yards long and is over almost as soon as it starts. One misjudged step along the way will ruin your chances. This runner, having cleared all barriers, will now use a sprint stride in his drive to the tape.

Joel Shankle (above) of the U.S.A. wins his heat at the 1956 Olympic Games. He has a clear lead on the rest of the field, showing his nation's superiority in the event. An examination of the form of the trailing athletes shows why American runners have dominated the hurdles. The runner to the left of Shankle has his lead leg bending to the left instead of pointing straight ahead as it leaves the ground. Compare the form of these athletes in general with that of the runners trailing Dillard on page 82 and pick out other errors of form.

Glenn Davis (left) clears the last barrier on his way to winning the 400-

meter event at the A.A.U. meets. Davis, normally a quarter-miler, at one time held the world's record for both the 440-yard flat race and the 400-meter hurdles.

The hurdles in a 400-meter race are placed 35 meters apart with the first one 45 meters from the starting line and the last one 40 meters from the finish. Competitors use thirteen or fifteen steps between hurdles, but must be prepared to clear with either leg leading as it is not always possible to maintain an exact measurement of steps in such a tiring event.

Here is a rare dead heat in the hurdles (below) between Lee Calhoun, left, and Jack Davis at the 1956 American Olympic tryouts. Once over the last hurdle, the athletes sprint as hard as they can for the tape. However, they must be sure that they do not start their sprint before they have their full balance after clearing the hurdle.

In their haste to reach the tape, both Calhoun and Davis are leaning a little too far forward so that their head and neck, rather than their chest, will hit the line first.

This was possibly the greatest high hurdle race ever run as Calhoun, Davis, Milt Campbell (right) and Elias Gilbert (not shown) were all at one time holders or co-holders of one of the world's hurdle records.

A hurdler, because of the various skills needed for his event, is often a great all-round athlete as well. Campbell, for instance, won the 1956 Olympic decathlon title. A boy who has tried other events with only fair success might therefore find his real specialty in the hurdles.

Penn State's anchor man takes baton from teammate for final run in the four-mile relay championship at the Penn Relays in Franklin Field, Philadelphia. The Penn State team was so far out in front that they bewildered their opponents to the point of head-scratching. This display of all out effort brought a new relay carnival record of 17:11.3 to the victors.

Relays

Among the most popular track and field events are the relays, for these allow more boys to participate in each race and also add excitement in the swift baton exchanges.

Almost all relay races are run by four-man teams, no matter what the distance of the event might be. The most common relays are the 440, 880, mile, two-mile and four-mile, in which each member of the team runs one-fourth of the total distance; and the sprint and distance medley relays, in which each man runs a different distance than his teammates.

The relay season is in April and early May and gives the athletes a chance to work gradually into top condition for the individual events in the late spring and summer months. Some relay carnivals, like the Penn and Drake Relays, are among the most important meets in a track and field season.

The most important thing for a relay runner to remember is that it is the baton that runs the race, not the boys who carry it. A boy who finishes a relay race without the baton is automatically disqualified. A team which drops the baton during a race must retrieve it, losing precious yards in the process.

The baton must always be carried in the hand and must be passed to the next runner within a 20-yard zone. If either of these rules is broken, the team is disqualified.

There are two major types of baton passes with minor variations of each.

One is the "blind pass," used in sprint relays like the 440 and 880; the other is the "visual pass" used in longer relays.

In the blind pass, the boy receiving the baton does not look back when it is placed in his hands. The timing for this pass must be perfect and this requires endless hours of practice. Sprint relays are won and lost on the baton exchanges.

The visual pass allows the athlete to look back as he takes the baton and is a slower, if surer, way of passing it.

No matter which baton pass is used, there are certain general rules which must be followed.

First of these is that the baton pass should be made with the two runners as far apart as possible, each one fully extending his arm — one forward, the other back — to make the connection. In a perfect pass, the runners will be about two yards apart and these are two yards their team will not have to run in carrying the baton to the finish line. These two yards could win the race.

Second rule is that the burden of a good baton pass is almost entirely upon the receiver. The boy with the baton has his own problems running the race. He may be quite tired as he approaches his teammate, so the receiver must never make the mistake of starting too soon and running away without the baton.

To be sure of a perfect pass, he should wait at the back edge of the passing zone, wave to the incoming runner until he is sure the boy sees him, then time his start so that he will take the baton in full stride at the proper distance. Starting too late is as bad as starting too soon, for then the incoming runner may catch up with him and wind up passing the baton sidewards or even backwards.

In a sprint relay, the baton pass should use up about 15 or 17 yards of the 20-yard zone. For longer relays, the distance gets progressively shorter until, in the four-mile relay (where each boy runs a mile) it is made in three or four yards.

Here is a baton pass in a high-school one-mile relay at the Penn Relays (opposite). With 14 or 15 teams in the race, this is a real test of baton passing. Of the five teams pictured, three are in various stages of good baton passes, two are not doing so well.

The boy wearing "C-2" shows the proper stance when waiting for a team-mate to come in. Because of the crowded conditions, he has stepped a couple of yards ahead of the back line and is turned back, arm outstretched with for-ward foot pointing ahead and rear foot sidewise.

Now look at the boy wearing "M-6." His teammate is arriving, so he starts running, both feet pointing ahead, but his body is still twisted so he can look back for the baton. His arm is also out-stretched.

At top, the boys wearing "F-1" and "F-2" complete a perfect pass. Both arms are fully outstretched and they are at least two yards apart. Notice that the baton pass is made from right hand to left hand. It could also be made left to

right, but never from right to right or from left to left, for these last two would force the incoming boy to run directly at his teammate, rather than to one side, and they could easily trip over each oth-er's legs.

The boys wearing "L-1" and "L-2" have just completed a left hand to left hand pass. The incoming runner has had to stop dead to avoid knocking down his teammate and they have thus lost the entire advantage of a running baton pass. Compare their distance apart with that of the team at top.

Finally, there is the team just below the top where the incoming runner is falling down as he hands off the stick. The mistake here is that the receiver did not take into account the hard race his teammate had run and started off too fast. He then had to stop, turn back and just manage to grab the baton before the other boy hit the ground. But, in-stead of being touched off even with the leader, he will be yards behind by the time he turns around and starts running.

The boy waiting for the baton should always hold his arm as steady as possible, even when running, so that he does not present a moving target to his teammate. The incoming runner should also, in his last stride or two, extend his arm in-stead of pumping it at the side. The re-ceiver's hand should be extended palm up so that a juggled baton has less chance of falling to the ground.

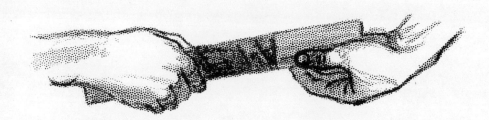

Receiver looks back, times start so pass can be made within exchange zone lines.

Blind Pass. — The sequence on this and the next page show two runners performing a blind pass to perfection.

Many sprint relays are won or lost between the exchange zone lines, so study the proper technique well and practice passing and receiving until you bcome smooth and efficient.

The receiver has waited until he is sure that the incoming runner is close enough and moving fast enough to catch up with him, then has turned and started his run. He drives straight forward, right arm beginning to reach back for the baton.

Since all sprint relays are run in lanes all the way around the track, the receiver would have to keep his eyes forward if only to be sure that he did not run out of his lane. Since it is also impossible to run at top speed if you can't see where you are going, the blind pass becomes a necessity. The idea of a sprint relay is that the man with the baton is always traveling as fast as he can from the moment he receives it to the moment he hands it off.

Receiver drops right arm back after three starting strides.

Hold receiving arm steady to give passer a still target.

Passer drives at top speed until pass is completed.

90

Passer reaches for target.

Receivers hand; palm up, fingers together forming open V with thumb.

Passer; grip baton tight on back end.

Passer guides baton into target with force.

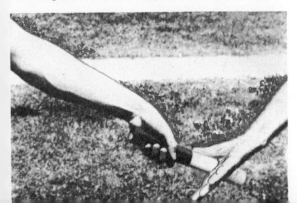

Passer does not let go.

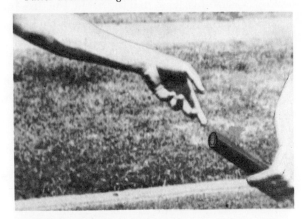

Receiver pulls baton from passer.

Pass complete, both runners at near top speed.

91

Passer slowing up, receiver speeds off.

Visual Pass. — The sequence on these two pages are excellent for viewing and studying the proper techniques of visual baton passing. Again, it is important to practice each phase of both passing and receiving until your ability is fine and polished.

The receiver is moving straight ahead with his legs, driving well, but his body is turned and arm extended back to receive the baton. He has not moved too soon, for the incoming runner will be able to catch him in another four or five strides, at about the end of the passing zone.

In longer relays, where the visual pass is used, the best strategy is for the receiver to get the baton as soon as possible without any loss of speed on the exchange. If the incoming runner is finishing strong, the pass may take 10 to 12 yards; if he is coming in slowly, the exchange can be made in two or three yards.

The idea is for the fresh man to get the baton and start running as soon as possible. If his team is ahead, he can pick up extra yards as the tired incoming runners of the other teams come home. If his team is behind, he can start chasing the leader, who has been opening up extra yardage in the same manner.

Coaches normally use their fastest starter on the opening, or leadoff, leg of a relay team, their best runner on the fourth, or anchor leg. If the leadoff man is a weak finisher, the second best runner will run the second leg; otherwise, he will usually run the third leg with the slowest man on the second leg. Of course,

Receiver strides off, peering over right shoulder, upper body slightly sidewise.

Receiver's right arm extended back to form target with right hand.

Passer, in full flight, reaches for target.

92

Receiver's right hand, palm up, fingers slightly spread ready for contact.

Passer, with firm grip on back end of baton, is ready to slap it into target.

Passer slaps baton into receiver's hand, forces fingers to start gripping.

Passer holds on to baton.

With a light grip.

Until receiver slips it out of his hand.

With baton firmly in hand,

Receiver turns head and body forward.

And turns on full speed as passer starts to break stride.

this strategy only is good in relays where each man runs the same distance. In medley relays, the coach simply uses the strongest man at each of the distances involved.

A danger to be avoided in the longer relays when a team falls far behind is that a boy may try to make up too much distance too soon. Without another runner near to guide by, and in an effort to catch up with the leaders, he will run all out in the first half of the race, then have nothing left for the last half. No matter where he is touched off, well ahead or well behind, the runner should pace himself just as he would in an individual race.

The receiver (opposite page) has taken the baton and has already switched it to his right hand, while the incoming runner is slowing up but continuing to run straight ahead. The baton should always be moved to the passing hand immediately after receiving it, otherwise the runner might forget to make the switch in the heat of competition. The incoming runner, particularly in sprint relays, should always continue on a straight course until he stops running, then look around to be sure he does not interfere with another team as he turns to walk off the track.

Here are views of the longest relay race, the four-mile event (above and be-

low). In this event, baton passing is completely secondary to the condition and ability of the athlete. The runners must just be sure that each pass is made safely and smoothly. They may also, if they wish, move the baton from one hand to another in the course of the race, lest one arm get tired from carrying it.

All of the teams make a visual pass (below). Note the full extension of the arms on the team at left, as compared with the close position of the team in back of them. The incoming runners finished almost together, but a better pass allows the leaders to take off with a two-yard advantage. In a shorter event, this could be important.

A baton exchange (below) in the 400-meter relay at the 1956 Olympic Games. The form on the team in the foreground is poor. The runners are much too close together at the point of exchange so that the left feet of the two men are side-by-side. Also, the receiver is taking the baton with palm of the hand down, a method that does not allow for full extension of his arm and that only experienced runners can use without risk of a dropped baton.

Notice that both teams are making the baton pass from left to right hand on the turn. This allows the receiving runner to stay close to the white line which marks the inside of his lane. A right to left hand pass would tend to force him to the outside and make him run an extra yard or two.

Though the team in the foreground appears to be leading here, actually the edge is due to the staggered start used for all sprint relays and will be lost when the runners complete the turn. To tell how a sprint relay from staggered starts is progressing, watch each baton pass and see which team exchanges the baton first.

Ron Delaney (below) takes the baton from Alex Breckenridge on the way to a distance medley relay victory at the Penn Relays. Delaney was without doubt the greatest performer in the history of this meet, which invented the relay race in the 1890s. In four years, he ran on ten winning teams in ten tries — one fresh-man and three varsity mile relays, three varsity sprint medley relays and three varsity distance medley relays.

The distances on the various medley legs are: sprint — 440 yards, 220 yards and 880 yards; distance — 880 yards, 440 yards, 1320 yards and one mile.

Field Techniques

Field events are sometimes called the "side show" of the sport of track and field. This is not so because a jumper — broad and high — a pole vaulter, shot-putter, etc., all must train just as rigorously and perform with the same degree of efficiency as those athletes who make up the running part of the program.

The competitors entered in the field events find that there is no easy way to success. Although a field competitor — particularly a weight man — is usually stronger and taller than the sprint or distance runner, this does not mean that a slightly-built boy of medium height and weight, who wants to compete in the field events, should feel discouraged. Any boy who has the desire and competitive drive to be a field man should certainly · try his hand at one of these events. Only through competition can a future ath-

lete determine his true value as a participant.

Those competing in field events usually do not get the attention they deserve simply because they are performing their specialties while the runners are doing theirs. However, the true athlete is one who wants to compete for the satisfaction of pitting his skill against an opponent — and outdoing him. Everything else is secondary.

You heavier boys in the field events who are sometimes kidded by your friends for your slowness afoot should derive pleasure from the fact that you are making use of your God-given skills in the best possible manner. Never feel embarrassed that you cannot run in the 100 or 220; the sprint man may have a secret ambition to throw the hammer or put the shot.

Broad Jump

This is an event which requires speed, springy legs and a certain amount of agility. Most broad jumpers are also sprinters, though others combine this event with the high jump or pole vault.

A broad jump layout consists of a hard-packed runway about 40 or 50 yards long, leading to a take-off board sunk flush with the ground and to a soft landing pit about 25 feet in length. The take-off board may be 24 inches wide for high-school competition, but only eight inches wide for college and A.A.U. meets.

Few athletes specialize solely in the broad jump until they enter college. At that time, sprinters who are not of championship class, but who have the proper physical requirements for the broad jump, will begin to really concentrate on the event.

Broad jumpers come in all shapes and sizes. Some are tall and thin, others of medium height and build and still others are short and stocky. Some have more speed than spring, others more spring than speed and a rare few, like Olympic champion Jesse Owens, perfectly combine the two.

The magic mark for broad jumpers is 26 feet, a distance achieved by very few athletes in the history of track and field. Most college athletes feel satisfied if they can better 24 feet and the average college jumper will do between 22 and 24 feet.

In high school, it takes a jump of over 22 feet to win most major meets and some remarkable high-school athletes have leaped more than 25 feet. In elementary school, a jumper should be content with leaps of 13 to 17 feet, depending on his age, size and experience.

Broad jumpers, in practice drills, seldom leap for distance except in competition. Their training consists of calisthenics for loosening the muscles, sprinting, high jump practice and easy jumps into the pit which emphasize form and height, not distance.

The broad jump can be broken down into four steps, each of which must be mastered by a champion: 1. the approach, 2. the takeoff, 3. the glide through the air, 4. the landing.

Of these four, the one most neglected by the majority of beginning jumpers is the approach. This is not just the simple matter of sprinting down the runway and taking off for a jump. It requires a great deal of preparation each time a jumper competes.

The reason for this is that jumps are measured from the front edge of the take-off board to the nearest mark made by the competitor. A jumper who takes off from behind the front of the board gets no credit for the extra distance jumped. And one who goes beyond the board commits a foul and receives no credit at all for that jump.

Moreover, an athlete will not reach the full potential of his jump, merely by making sure that his toe hits the front of the board on each takeoff. He must also be traveling at top speed when he arrives there: neither reaching forward nor cutting his stride to hit the mark. Either of these tactics will slow him down at the crucial moment of takeoff.

To assure a proper takeoff, a competitor must measure off his approach precisely so that he will be able to hit the front edge of the board on every jump.

This is done by measuring off a distance equivalent to the number of strides he intends to use on his approach, allowing about five and a half feet for each stride. For a 16-stride approach, this will be about 95 feet. When the measurement has been made, a marker should be placed there.

Placing his take-off foot on the mark, the jumper then runs through an approach, having teammates note and mark where his foot lands on the second and eighth step. If this first run carries him to the edge of the board on his 16th step, he is ready to try a jump. If his measurement is off, adjustments must be made until his marks are properly placed.

The running approach of 16 steps allows two steps to hit full stride, six more to reach top speed and the final eight to build up momentum for the takeoff.

The running stride used in the broad jump is the same as in sprinting (opposite page). Knees are brought high and arms pump vigorously. However, the last three steps before the takeoff are more relaxed, though with no lessening of speed. And the final step or two should be slightly shorter than the others.

Should the jumper need more of a run to hit top speed, he can extend his approach to 18, 20 or even 22 steps. Some jumpers also prefer to trot up to the first mark before starting the actual run.

It was mentioned previously that part of a broad jumper's training schedule involves work over the high jump bar. This is because getting enough height is such an important part of the broad jump. Beginners make the mistake of leaping straight forward into the pit, instead of taking off both upward and forward. As a result, they get very little distance.

To insure a proper takeoff, the body must be practically erect when the take-off foot hits the board (a very slight forward lean is permissible). This is the reason for the shorter strides before take-off — to allow the body to catch up with the legs. Should the body be either too far forward of too far back, the jump would be spoiled.

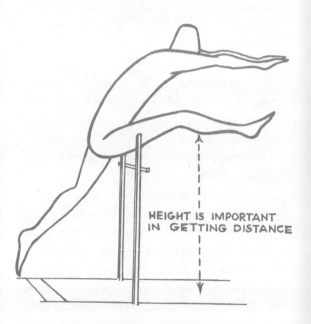

HEIGHT IS IMPORTANT IN GETTING DISTANCE

A good exercise to improve height.

The Takeoff. — This picture (above), shows correct take-off form. The left foot is driving the body off the ground as the right knee lifts high to carry it into the air. Arms and heads swing toward the sky to help the upward movement.

A jumper may use either foot on the takeoff, choosing whichever feels most natural to him.

Coming In. — As the jumper approaches the landing (below), the legs have swung forward to squeeze the last extra inch out of the jump. The arms also begin to move forward to aid the balance at the impact of landing. Many good jumps are spoiled when the jumper's legs get too far in front of him so that he loses balance and falls back on his haunches.

The legs must be relaxed for the landing, otherwise the athlete could be injured.

Airborne. — At the peak of his jump, the athlete has his back arched, arms flung upward. His legs are carried in a sitting position, ready to be flung forward for the landing (opposite).

There are varying styles of carrying the legs through the air and we shall see other examples on pages 106 and 107. But all have the same purpose: to keep the jumper in the air as long as possible.

Bringing the legs into this position and holding them there requires strong abdominal muscles, which can only be developed through calisthenics.

Landing. — This is a perfect landing (below). The back is erect and the head and arms are leaning forward. Feet are spread about a foot apart to help balance the body as it prepares to fall forward. The chin has come down to the chest and the arms are ready to swing backward to aid the forward motion.

On longer jumps, an athlete may have to swing his body forward vigorously at the moment of landing to prevent a backward fall. The longer the jump, the more need for precise balance at all times.

105

Another style of carrying the body through the air in the broad jump is shown (left) by champion pole-vaulter Bob Gutowski. He uses the sitting position, but with knees tucked against the chest and arms extended straight forward. His body is bent forward and eyes are on the ground.

Some competitors prefer the "hitch-kick" or running in air style (right). The lead leg is extended forward, then swung backward while the take-off leg comes forward. It amounts to taking a step in mid-air. The lead leg then rejoins the take-off leg in front of the body for the landing. Arms are extended to the side and the body has only a slight forward lean.

This style (right) is halfway between the sitting and the "hitch-kick." The body is almost erect and the arms are flung overhead. Notice that the shoe worn by this jumper has spikes on both sole and heel. This is called a jumper's shoe and is usually worn only for the high jump and pole vault.

The jumper (left) employs the kneeling style in which both legs are brought behind the body after the takeoff, then flung forward sharply in an effort to gain added inches on the landing. Arms are flung to the side and the back is arched. The problem in this jump is to maintain balance on the landing, as the forward thrust of the legs makes a backward fall very possible.

High Jump

The high jump offers an athlete the greatest variety of techniques of any field event. There are three major styles of jumping — the scissors kick, the Eastern Roll and the Western Roll — and each of these has so many variations that, in a way, every high jumper can be said to have his own individual style.

High jumpers are generally tall and lanky, though there have been some fine jumpers who were no more than six feet tall, if indeed that big. A boy who is not too tall but has a desire to high jump should not let a lack of size interfere. High jumpers *do not* have to be six feet or taller. The chief physical requisite is a pair of strong, springy legs with bodily coordination running a close second.

A high jumping layout includes a fan-shaped approach of hard dirt; a pair of standards placed 12 feet apart to support the cross bar and the landing pit, which should measure 16 feet across and be 12 feet deep.

There are no restrictions on how a jumper must clear the bar, so long as he uses only one foot for the takeoff. He is given three tries at each height and the bar is moved up one or two inches at a time.

The original method of clearing the bar, used by all athletes until 1895, was the scissors kick. In that year, Mike Sweney introduced the Eastern Roll; in 1912, George Horine first displayed the Western Roll.

Each change of style resulted in an improvement in the world's record until the magic mark of seven feet was cleared for the first time by Charles Dumas in 1956. Several Russian athletes followed Dumas into the seven-foot class, using a controversial built-up jumping shoe which was outlawed in 1958. A seventeen-year old Boston University student, John Thomas, became the second American seven-footer in 1959. In June 1960 Thomas set a new outdoor record of seven feet-three and three quarter inches during the Olympic Trials at Palo Alto, California. The picture on the opposite page shows Thomas going over the bar at this fantastic record height.

The six-foot level is the target for most high-school athletes, but boys like Thomas and Dumas cleared six-foot eight or better while still in school. A fair college or A.A.U. jumper does six-foot, four, a good one, six-foot, six and a champion six foot eight or better.

More than any other event, the high jump requires supreme confidence on the part of the athlete. He must "know" that he is going to clear the bar, or he shouldn't even bother to jump. It takes a special brand of confidence when a jumper faces a bar which is six or seven inches, or even more, over his own height.

Training for the high jump includes exercises to strengthen the legs and add to their spring. The great Russian jumpers were the first to use weight-lifting and Thomas adopted it prior to his seven-foot jumps.

Otherwise, a high jumper should spend time on improving his general body coordination. He must run at every practice to increase his speed. Normally, a jumper competes in other events as well — usually the hurdles, broad jump or pole vault — and practice in these events will assist this program.

The scissors kick is used only by beginners and should be discarded as soon as the jumper has learned to roll. For the scissors, the athlete approaches the bar from the right, if he is right-handed, at an angle of only ten or fifteen degrees. His right leg thrusts up and he springs off the left. The legs cross the bar, one after the other, with the jumper in a sitting position.

The Eastern Roll, used chiefly by European jumpers, has the athlete approach the bar almost head on. His last two steps turn his right side toward the bar and the right leg again leaves the ground first. The leg motion is similar to that of the high hurdles, but with the body leaning back so that he clears the bar in a horizontal position.

Almost all American jumpers use some variation of the Western Roll. The orthodox style, as introduced by Horine, has the right-handed athlete approach the bar from the left at a 45-degree angle. He takes off from his left leg, with the right leg leading, and clears the bar with his left side toward the ground, left leg tucked under the right.

This style prevailed until the 1930s when the variation known as the "straddle" caught on. The takeoff is the same, but the right leg kicks more vigorously and leads the body over the bar in a face-down position. This is the style used by Dumas and Thomas to clear seven feet.

For his running approach, the high jumper uses seven or eight steps, the first few slow and bouncy, the last few faster and longer. He needs only two checkmarks, one for his take-off foot at arm's length from the cross bar and the other for his start, about 30-35 feet from the first mark. A few practice runs to the bar will locate the latter point.

The success or failure of each jump usually depends, not on what an athlete does while up in the air, but on how he leaves the ground. His jumping action should be as vertical as possible — no effort should be wasted on unnecessary horizontal movement. And he should

avoid the mistake of leaning into the jump with his upper body.

Many jumpers like to try the lower heights with their sweatsuits on, then take them off as the bar goes higher. This way, they get a little extra confidence being able to clear the bar with the suits on, so that when they take them off they automatically feel they should increase their jump by several inches. Actually, it is better to skip the early jumps and save energy by making all jumps with sweatshirts off.

Robert Shavlakadze, below, of the U.S.S.R. team, is shown clearing the bar at seven feet-one inch to capture the high jump gold medal in the 1960 Olympics at Rome, Italy. Shavlakadze, a surprise winner when John Thomas of the U.S. failed to live up to his advance notices as the greatest high jumper ever, barely nosed out teammate Valeriy Brumel.

On these pages is pictured the jumping style of Dwight Eddleman, former Olympian, using the orthodox, or side-down Western Roll.

Eddleman, left, finishes measuring off the distance for his running approach. Experienced jumpers know precisely the length of their run and can measure it off with a tape, then test the marks by taking a practice jump.

Eddleman is the picture of concentration at lower left as he gets ready for his running approach. He gazes directly at the bar, pauses to settle his nerves and then goes into the run-up. Nothing should be allowed to disturb a jumper's concentration once he has started for the bar and it is a wise athlete who early learns how to shut out crowd noises from his ears.

At the moment of take-off, right, Eddleman is leaning well back away from the bar, body weight behind his left leg and the right leg swinging forward for the take-off. Like many jumpers, he has a blind spot at this point (his eyes are actually closed), but they will open again as he leaves the ground. This is the moment of supreme physical effort for the jumper as the tense muscles of both arms and legs show.

To avoid the upper body lean into the bar, a beginner can make his foot plant at almost a right angle to the bar. This way, the body will lean backward, directly away from the bar at the moment of takeoff. There is little chance then, that the head and shoulders will get ahead of the leg on the jump.

The kick of the right leg should not be at the bar, but rather at the standard on the right side and almost parallel to the bar. This will also help to prevent the body lean at takeoff.

Coming up to the bar (opposite), his right leg is straightening out and the left is going into the tucked position in which it will be carried over the bar. The right arm is flung up and out and the left is bent at the elbow as it goes past the bar. His eyes are squarely on target again.

In the final moment before clearance (above) his right arm has turned up with fist clenched as if to help give a final lift and his left arm is extended straight out. The right leg is now almost straight and practically parallel with the bar, while the left is bent tightly at the knee and moving closer to its final position under the right. The upper body also comes forward toward his leg, twisting so that he will be turned over on his side at the proper moment.

A perfect layout of the orthodox Western Roll (below). Both hands point straight forward and the left arm is held high so there is no danger of it hitting the bar. The left leg is up under the right. The head begins to drop down as the body strains to lift the hips over the bar. A slight back kick with the right leg at this point will also help the hips to clear.

As good as this form is, it should be easy to see how higher jumps are achieved with the straddle. By turning the body to face down at the point of clearance, the athlete does not have the problem of getting both legs and both hips over the bar simultaneously. Put another way, the body is thinner from back to front than from side to side and those extra inches mean a higher jump for the same amount of lifting effort.

115

Starting in the lower left corner and looking up, over, then down, this sequence of pictures shows the straddle-style of the Western Roll. This style of high jumping has become most popular in all age groups throughout the world.

The jumper (left) plants his left foot for the spring. His body weight is now leaning backward and will only come directly over the take-off foot when he is ready to leave the ground. The right knee is bent on the swing forward, but will straighten out on the vigorous kick-up.

Both arms should help with the take-off by lifting up. The left foot should hit heel first and, as the athlete kicks up with the right leg, his body rocks forward onto the ball of his left foot. Because of this heel-first plant of the left foot, athletes usually wear a jumping shoe, with two spikes in the heel to grip the ground.

To avoid the upper body lean into the bar, a beginner can make his foot plant at almost a right angle to the bar. This way, the body will lean backward, directly away from the bar at the moment of takeoff. There is little chance then, that the head and shoulders will get ahead of the leg on the jump.

The kick of the right leg should not be at the bar, but rather at the standard on the right side and almost parallel to the

bar. This will also help to prevent the body lean at takeoff.

Though most jumpers have a tendency to go directly into the straddle-style of the Western Roll from the scissors, it is better if they first learn the orthodox style, as the proper takeoff is more natural this way. A jumper should always hit the ground with one foot and two hands simultaneously. Allowing the body weight to be borne only by the arms can result in an injury, even in a soft pit. The right leg in proper position will bear its share of the shock of the landing. With the orthodox style, it is the left leg, tucked under the right, which hits the ground first.

Why is this so? Remember that the body goes over with side down. Therefore the right shoulder goes over even with the left and there is no way for it to lead the rest of the body. Even if a jumper intends to use the straddle style as his permanent form, he can start with the orthodox style, perfect his takeoff, and then switch to the straddle, there being so little difference in the two methods until after the jumper leaves the ground.

Normally, with the body in a straight layout over the bar, the right leg acts as a counterbalance to the left, going down toward the pit as the left leg comes up over the bar.

A "front view" sequence on these two pages shows the straddle-style as used by a "power" jumper, J. Lewis Hall, at an indoor meet. Like many shorter jumpers, Hall needed greater leg spring and a higher kick with the right leg to get him over a height such as the six foot, seven and one-half inches he clears in these photos. Power jumpers usually achieve their best marks at indoor meets where the wood surface affords more spring than the dirt approach of outdoor tracks.

Hall kicks high (above) with his right leg and more directly at the bar than the average jumper. His arms are also flung high to help the upward motion, but the left one is ready to drop down and back to help the body make its turn over the bar.

Thus we see, at upper left, that the left leg has begun to straighten out, while the right leg does its part in tipping the body over the bar by starting down toward the pit. The right arm also comes down while the left arm is swung up and back to help continue the body's turn.

Above, the leg is fully extended as Hall starts falling to the pit. His margin of clearance is narrow, but sufficient. The violence of his spring has enabled him to clear a height several inches over his own head.

Contrast the leg position above, with that of Eddleman at a similar stage of his jump in the previous sequence. Hall's legs are widely separated and will stay that way. His left arm is now swinging out behind the body as he turns toward the bar.

He starts over the bar with the right leg and arm leading the body (above center). It would seem impossible at this point for him to lift the left leg over, but the twisting motion of his body and a simple straightening of the knee joint will take care of that detail.

Power jumpers usually find their landings a little harder than the taller, more graceful boys. Hall's right arm, above, leads his right leg to the pit and will bear the brunt of the first impact. But, with the arm fully extended, there is no chance that it will be caught under the body and possibly injured.

It is probable that even greater refinements will be brought to the Western Roll in the future. Thomas has already made one change in that his body twist is so great that he does a complete turn and lands flat on his back. He has also cut his run-up to just four strides.

Another of the great power jumpers, all-round athlete Irving Mondschein (above), shown trying for six foot, nine inches. More noted as a decathlon performer, Mondschein was no more than six feet tall. He was also a left-hander, so this sequence presents the high jump from a different angle.

The style is again the straddle, but with an extreme upper body lean toward the bar, rare at such great heights.

Mondschein comes up to the bar, with right leg extended and left knee slightly bent. Note that he keeps his right arm close to his side, unlike Hall, and that the legs are also much closer together. The latter is due to the fact that the head, not the arm and leg, is leading him over the bar.

Mondschein (below) starts down for the pit. Every part of his body, except the right leg, is over. But, because the upper body has gotten too far ahead of the leg, he does not have the proper balance at

this point to lift that leg or straighten it out, so it tips the bar as it comes over.

Note the tenseness of the arm and leg muscles (above) as Mondschein heads down toward the pit. The falling left leg has now managed to balance the right one high into the air, but it is too late to save the jump. The landing will also be a hard one, as neither left arm nor leg is in position to break the fall. He hits the pit (below), head and elbow first, with the bar tumbling down atop him.

Mondschein's style of jumping was unorthodox as he mixed the leg motion of the straddle with the arm motion of the orthodox Western Roll, but it suited his abilities. There is a lesson in this for all high jumpers. Try the various styles to find the one that suits you best, then adapt it to your own physical characteristics. High jumping is one event where the competitors, not the coaches, have pioneered the changes in style over the years.

The fabulous John Thomas (right) winning the national interscholastic title at six feet, seven and five-eighth inches. No style perfectionist at this early stage, Thomas leads with his head over the bar.

Walter Davis (left), who pushed the world's record to six feet, eleven and one-half inches, displays the orthodox Western Roll. Davis overcame the handicap of a severe polio attack in his youth.

Eddleman is shown (right) clearing a low height. He has straightened his right leg after passing the bar and his left arm reaches down for the landing.

The Eastern Roll (left) as practiced by Olympic champion John Winter of Australia. Left leg leads over the bar as the right leg follows. High position of the body proves this style inferior.

The orthodox Western Roll (right) as done by a left-hander. Position of arms and legs is simply reversed. Note the extreme lean of his head downward as the hips swing up over the bar.

An unusual view of the orthodox Western Roll (left) from below the jumper. This is imperfect form as the head leads over the bar. This athlete has great spring, but is not making the most of it.

Women high jumpers use the same form as men, but their best leaps are about one foot lower. The event is a dangerous one for girls and should be practiced under the supervision of an experienced coach.

Most girls will start off using the scissors kick, but they should be changed to either the Eastern or Western roll as soon as possible. Not only will they jump higher, but they will also avoid jarring landings on their back, which could be both painful and dangerous.

Above, and at opposite, below, are two jumpers using the Eastern roll. Notice the grace of the girl above and contrast it with the awkwardness of the girl at right. It's worth noting, too, that the girl in the above photo is clearing a height just one foot above that accomplished by the other jumper.

Above, is a girl using the Western roll. Her style is comparable to that of the men jumpers shown on previous pages. Oddly, though, the best women jumpers use the Eastern roll and find they can go higher with this style than with the Western roll preferred by all top men jumpers.

Pole Vault

While youngsters of average size have been somewhat successful in this sport, the tall boys have been more successful over a period of time.

A pole vault layout looks something like the one used for the broad jump. There is a runway of about 150 feet of hard-packed dirt, leading to the pit, which is about 16 feet wide and 12 feet deep. Just before the pit there is an open wood or metal box set in the ground, called the vaulting box. And on either side of this box, about twelve feet apart, stand the two uprights which support the cross bar.

Like the high jump, the pole vault is an event for tall athletes although average-size vaulters have competed, and excelled. No world championship vaulter since 1920 has been shorter than five foot, ten and most are an inch or two over six feet.

The vaulter must have great arm and shoulder strength, acrobatic ability, good running speed and springy legs. He must, in other words, be a fine all-round athlete, also adept at other events.

The poles used are made of aluminum, bamboo, steel or glass, with the last two being most common. They come in varying sizes and weights and a beginner should choose a pole which he can comfortably handle. A vaulter wears jumping shoes in competition, though sometimes with only one spike in each heel.

Boys should not try to pole vault until they have entered high school and can learn under the eyes of an experienced coach, as this can be a dangerous event. Good high-school vaulters can clear 11 feet, with some champions going as high as 13 or even 14 feet. College and A.A.U. vaulters aim at the 15-foot mark, with the very best clearing heights close to 16 feet.

A vaulter should begin his training in the gymnasium, doing handstands, climbing rope and working out on the parallel bars to strengthen his arms and shoulders. He should also spend some time on the track trying to increase his running speed, as champion vaulters must attain a speed equal to an 11-second, 100-yard dash in their running approach.

The first item of business when the beginner tries actual vaulting is to choose his grip on the pole. A right-handed boy places his right hand higher than his left, a southpaw does just the opposite. But the important decision is just how far to place the hands from the front (or lower) end of the pole.

A good rule of thumb for beginners is to place the back hand about one foot higher on the pole than the height of the cross bar he will attempt to clear. Thus, if the bar is at seven feet, the right hand (or left, as the case may be) will be eight feet from the forward end.

12 FOOT MARK

11 FEET

127

The picture below shows the correct position of the hands on the pole as the vaulter stands at rest before starting his run. The right hand is slightly behind the body and grips the pole with palm up. The left is about eighteen inches away and grips the pole with palm down. When the vaulter lifts the pole to start his run, the left hand will move forward until it is almost three feet from the right hand.

Just as in the broad jump, the athlete must precisely measure his running approach. He first must find his take-off mark by placing the front end of the pole in the vaulting box and extending the pole over his head with both hands. His body should be absolutely erect so that a straight line could join his right hand, back of his head and heels.

The mark can then be placed at the side of the runway, even with his toes. A right-handed vaulter will take off with his left foot so that the body can swing past the pole on the right side. A left-handed vaulter will take off from his left foot.

With the take-off mark set, the athlete proceeds to place his other marks just as in the broad jump. He must remember, however, to carry the pole when running through his approach to set these marks, otherwise they would be useless. The weight of the pole naturally affects the length of his stride (right).

With his take-off position set and his grip on the pole selected, the athlete is ready for some practice vaults. The six major points in the pole vault are: 1. running approach, 2. plant of the pole, 3. take-off, 4. swing and pull-up, 5. clearing the bar, and 6. landing.

The ideal is for a boy to reduce these six steps into one fluid motion. The spectator, watching an expert vaulter, seldom notices how many separate actions are involved, for his eye is caught by the great sweep of power as the athlete leaves the ground and soars over the bar.

Any jerky motion along the way will rob a vaulter of the power generated by his running approach and the combined action of his legs and shoulder muscles in lifting him off the ground. Unlike many athletic events, where too conscious of form, an athlete will hurt his effectiveness, in pole vaulting the two must go together.

This need for rhythm rests on the fact that the vaulter must combine the long heavy pole with the motion of his body, maintaining perfect balance at all time. This timing comes only after several years of work and even the experts must "warm up" before every meet to be sure that they are "in the groove."

Running Approach. — A beginner will take a running approach of about 95 yards, or 16 steps. Champions use an approach of as much as 150 yards. The pole is carried in one of two positions: at a slight angle to the ground with front end pointing upward, as seen right; or parallel to the ground.

The running stride should be that of a quarter-miler: knees must drive high, but body has to stay relaxed. The hands are about three feet apart and eyes looking straight ahead to the bar.

Planting the Pole. — If the pole is carried with front end up in the air, it will be planted in the box with an overhand thrust as seen right. If carried parallel, thrust is underhand. In either case, as the right arm moves the pole into position for the plant, it shoves it through the left, leaving the hands about eighteen inches apart. The front tip of the pole is placed on the V-shaped surface of the box and then slides forward until it jolts against the back end.

Takeoff. — At about the same moment that the pole hits the back end of the box, the left foot hits the ground for the take-off spring. This is quite like the takeoff in the broad jump, though not quite as strong, as the arms will help raise the body in this event. The knee is slightly bent at the takeoff and the foot should be in perfect line with the point of the pole, so that the whole momentum of both body and pole is directly forward. The right leg swings past the left to lead the body on its upward journey.

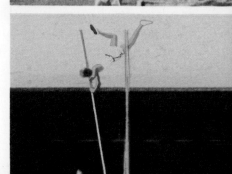

Clearing. — Two body positions are used in clearing the bar: the flyaway and the jackknife (at left). The flyaway is used on vaults where the handgrip is above or even with the cross bar. The vaulter allows his momentum to carry the body over the bar, then shoves the pole back with both hands. The jackknife is used when the grip is below the level of the cross bar. The vaulter drops his feet over the bar, still holding to the pole. He raises his hips, releases the left hand, then shoves off with his right to help carry his upper body over.

Landing. — The vaulter relaxes completely, with body extended, legs directly under his body and slightly bent at the knees so that his legs will accept the shock when hitting the pit. (Below.)

Swing and Pull-up. — The body swings forward as close to the pole as possible with knees drawn slightly up. When the hips are level with the shoulders (left), the arms begin their pull to bring the body into the position of a handstand on the pole. The vaulter pulls his body right along the pole, keeping legs tucked up so that the feet do not touch the bar as they go by. When the right leg reaches a point just above the bar, the left leg kicks vigorously upward and outward to reverse the body so that the vaulter is facing toward the pit.

131

On these two pages is a view of pole vaulting from another angle, directly behind the vaulter, who, in this case, is Bob Richards, two-time Olympic champion. During his long career, Richards set a record by clearing 15 feet in more than 100 meets.

Richards (above) is seen just after the takeoff. Note how his body seems about to swing right into the pole. There is no wasted motion to either side. His right arm is fully extended and his left bent, with the handgrips about one foot apart.

On the swing-up (middle), Richards' feet are together, the right only slightly higher than the left. His arms are ready to begin the pull and his eyes are on the target, the bar above. Notice the tremendous muscle development in his arms and shoulders.

He is halfway through the pull-up (below). The right foot is now definitely leading the left and the knee is bent so that it will not hit the bar. The hands are a little closer together at this point. Both elbows are bent and the great strain of lifting the body is shown in the tenseness of the shoulder muscles.

Notice that all the way through the swing and pull-up, the body stays close to the pole. Every bit of effort goes toward a direct vertical movement.

He is three-quarters through the pull-up (right). The right leg is now almost fully extended with the foot over the bar. The left leg is tucked up as it goes past the bar. The body has begun the reverse turn and is facing the pole.

The turn is practically complete (middle). The left leg has thrust out sharply to help the turn and the right knee is bent again to make sure that the foot does not come down on the bar.

This picture gives a good view of the handgrip. The hands, which were three feet apart on the running approach, are now no more than six inches apart and the right hand is about 12 feet, 6 inches high on the pole. The bar, in this case, is at 13 feet, 6 inches, so Richards' position in clearing is halfway between a flyaway and a jackknife.

Champion vaulters are able to grip the pole anywhere from 12 to almost 14 feet high, depending on their height and the speed with which they come down the runway.

Richards (below) has shoved off and is on his way down to the pit. Note that the left arm is held high so that the elbow will not brush the bar as it goes over. The right arm, which has given the final shove-off to the pole, is held in close to the body to avoid contact on the way down.

Indoor vaulting, such as pictured here, has the advantage of no wind or rain to hamper the athletes. But most arenas are too small to provide the 150-foot runway required by champions.

Don Bragg, 1960 Olympic Pole Vaulting champion with a record vault of fifteen feet-five inches is shown on these two pages in six wonderful sequence pictures clearing the bar at fifteen feet-four and one half inches to win the Chicago Daily News Relays.

In the seventeenth Olympic Games at Rome, Italy the pole vaulters went through two days of very rugged competition before Bragg became the first Olympic pole vaulter in history to clear the fifteen foot mark. He did so at 7:15 p.m. on the second day of competition as darkness began to settle over the huge arena.

After studying Bragg's feat in these pictures, it is easy to see why he has been listed as one of the outstanding pole vaulters of modern time. With more competition yet ahead of him, Bragg, still has his sights set on establishing a new world record, which is now fifteen feet-nine and three-quarters inches.

This vaulter (left) is not a specialist in the event as his form clearly shows. He has not been able to complete the handstand and his feet are already over the bar with body still facing the pole. Sheer strength is making the clearance possible. The vaulter is Jim Bausch, one of the all-time great decathlon stars.

In contrast, here is a champion vaulter, Don Laz, sailing over the bar in a flyaway at 13 feet, 11½ inches. His grip on the pole was more than thirteen feet high, which allowed this style of clearing on so high a vault. Laz was a 15-foot vaulter and was the one who introduced a style of carrying the pole across the body on the running approach.

Above is pictured a world's record jump of 15 feet, 8¼ inches by Bob Gutowski. His body clears the bar in a modified jackknife. The left arm is held up as it goes over and the right arm has just released the pole.

Note the strain in the neck and face muscles as his upper body struggles to clear the bar.

Richards (right) is seen on his way down to the pit after a 15-foot vault. He falls relaxed, but with eyes down to pick out a soft spot to land. Pole vault pits normally are piled higher with sawdust than this one. As in the vault on the preceding page (above), this one took place in a decathlon meet at which Richards won the national A.A.U. title.

Shot Put

At first glance, the shot put looks like the simplest event in track and field — little more than throwing a stone — but it is one which requires a great deal of practice before an athlete reaches championship class.

Shot-putters — while not necessarily — are usually the tallest and heaviest boys on the squad. But sheer strength is not enough in this event. The shot-putter must also have quick reflexes, good muscular coordination and the ability to explode his energy in one fast, hard move across the circle.

The shot put belongs to the class of weight events, which also includes the discus throw, javelin throw and hammer throw. Most athletes combine two or more of these events, the most normal "double" being the shot put and discus. However, some shot-putters also combine their event with the sprints or jumps.

Competition is held from a circle of seven-foot diameter with a four-inch high toeboard set flush with the putting side of the circle. The athlete must not touch the ground outside of the circle, nor step on the board, during his put. After the shot has left his hand, he must recover his balance, then leave from the back half of the circle.

The arm movement in the shot put must be a shove from the elbow and shoulder, rather than a throw. The hand cannot come outside of or behind the shoulder at any time during the put. To gain extra distance, the athlete uses a hop and a reverse twist of the body to carry him across the circle.

Junior shot-putters, in grade school or in freshman year of high school, put an eight-pound shot. In high school, the shot weighs twelve pounds, while in college and A.A.U. competition, it is sixteen pounds.

At all three levels of competition, a 45-foot toss is considered good, a 50-foot toss is very good and a 55-foot toss is excellent. The very best high school, college or A.A.U. shot-putters hit over 60 feet, a mark not reached with either the 12 or 16-pound shot until the 1950s.

The 60-foot put was made possible by a radical change in technique, plus the introduction of weight lifting to the training schedule. Two California athletes, Parry O'Brien and Otis Chandler, are generally credited with these innovations, which maintained America's traditional superiority in this event.

The technique used almost universally prior to 1950 saw the shot-putter stand with right side at the back of the circle and left side toward the front (or just the reverse if he was left-handed).

He went into a slight crouch, balancing on his right foot, took a short hop, then reversed the body to land with the left foot against the inside of the toeboard. At the same time, his arm shot up from his shoulder and let the ball go.

This is still the best style for beginners to use. The body movement is almost exactly the same as in the more advanced style pictured in the following pages. The difference is that it is easier to learn. A beginner, starting with the advanced style, would never develop a smooth move across the circle.

Weight lifting should be done only under the supervision of a coach and not until a boy has started putting the 12-pound shot. Heavy weights to build up the body are used in off-season, lighter weights when the athlete is in competition.

The explosive move of the shot-putter across the circle can be broken down into five parts: 1. the stance, 2. the crouch, 3. the hop, 4. the reverse, 5. the put and follow through.

Included in the stance is the proper grip of the shot and position of the arm. Two views are shown. Below is a shot-putter using the old style, preparatory to a sidewards move across the circle. At right is a shot-putter ready to use the new, backward move.

In each case, they hold the shot with fingers slightly spread so that it rests comfortably in the upper part of the hand. No part of the shot should rest on the palm of the hand itself, it should be no lower than the ridge which separates palm from fingers.

Notice the difference in the position of the arms in each case. The shot is tucked against the side of the neck and does not touch the chin (below). It is halfway between side and front and rests against the lower part of the chin (opposite).

The right arm in the photo (opposite) is well out from the side and the left arm is extended horizontally, to provide balance as the athlete drives across the circle.

In contrast, the athlete (above) holds the right arm closer to and more in front of his body and the left arm up in the air, also for balance.

The Stance. — A full-length view of the shot-putter (left) in his preliminary stance. He raises up on the toes of his right foot and the left leg is extended backwards for balance. Only when he is perfectly balanced in this position will he go into a crouch. The muscles of his right leg and arm are tense, but those of the left leg and arm should be as relaxed as possible. The body leans slightly forward and the putter is facing directly toward the back of the circle.

The Crouch. — In the photos below he has gone into the full crouch. Body is doubled up so that the right side of his chest lies on his right leg. Left arm and leg are still extended for balance, but his right foot is now fully planted and the right elbow has dropped so that the upper part of the arm is in a vertical position. If an athlete does not attain perfect balance on his first crouch, he can stand up and start all over again. An old-style shot-putter uses only a slight crouch and swings his left leg across his body before going into the hop. The left arm, in this case, is held as in the picture on the preceding page.

The Hop. — From this point on, the two styles are similar, differing only slightly in the positions of arms and legs. The hop is a very low one and, as seen in the last two pictures, the heel of the foot barely leaves the ground. The left arm has dropped toward the side, but the left leg is still extended, leading the way across the circle. An old-style shot-putter will start his hop as the left leg swings back toward the front of the circle and simply follow it across.

The hop must be carefully gauged, so that the shot-putter's left foot will not land on the toeboard for a foul when he reverses his body. The foot should land a few inches from the inside of the board and slide up to it as he comes around.

The body must be carried low on the hop, so that the force of the put will be upwards as well as forwards. Ideally, the shot should leave the hand with the right leg, side and arm in a straight line at a 45-degree angle to the ground. The impact of the put should start from the right heel and carry directly along that line, with the wrist giving it an extra push as it leaves the hand. Beginners usually get only their arm and shoulder behind the put and lose the benefit of their leg power by rising too suddenly from the crouch.

The Reverse. — As the hop is completed, the left leg swings around and down to the ground and the body makes its swift half-turn, bringing the punch up from the ground. The elbow drives upward right through the hand, as it were, and the shot leaves the fingers when the arm is fully extended. The shot-putter at right has completed his reverse and is about to let the ball go.

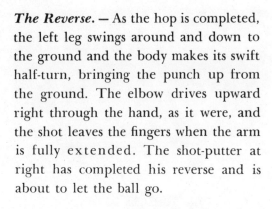

144

The Put and Follow Through. — The shot-putter follows through with left leg swinging back and right coming up to the board. A straight line could almost be drawn from the shot through the right arm and down through the body to the left foot. The left arm has completed the swing back it started in the hop and once again helps balance the body.

Because the women's shot is scaled down to their physical abilities, they are able to toss it as far as men do the 16-pound pellet. (A women's shot weighs about eight pounds.)

Above, Tamara Press of Russia gives a regular "Parry O'Brien" grunt as she heaves the pill 55 feet, 6¾ inches for a new world's record in a 1959 meet.

Opposite, Frances Kaszubski of the United States shows perfect follow-through form while tossing the shot at the 1948 Olympic Games.

Discus Throw

One of the oldest events in track and field, the discus throw has changed very little since it was first held in the ancient Olympic Games. Greek athletes scaled the discus while standing on a platform, and were scored for form as well as distance. The modern athlete throws it from an eight foot, two and one-half inch circle and is able to toss it much farther.

Like the shot put, the discus used in high school is smaller than the one used in college and A.A.U. competition. High-school athletes use a discus weighing 3 pounds, 9 ounces, while the college and A.A.U. discus weighs 4 pounds, 6.4 ounces.

The difference in weight allows the high-school thrower to achieve the same distances as the older athletes. In any level of competition, a throw of 130 feet is fair; 150 feet is good and 170 feet or better is excellent. The record for both weight implements is over 190 feet.

Many shot-putters also excel in the discus, but the physical requirements for the two events are not quite the same. In addition to a powerful pair of shoulders and legs, a discus thrower also needs a strong hand to control the platter and a long powerful arm with which to sling it.

Champion discus throwers usually stand over six feet tall and weigh over 190 pounds. But, on the high-school level, any boy can also excel in this event, provided he has proper muscular development.

Discus rules are very much like those of the shot put. The thrower must not touch any part of the rim of the circle or the ground outside of it during his throw. He must regain balance after the discus leaves his hand and leave the circle by the back half. There is, however, no toeboard at the front of the circle as in the shot put.

Weight lifting can play a part in the training of a discus thrower, just as it does for the shot-putter. But the athlete must try to develop long, wiry muscles in the upper arms, rather than short, bulky ones. This means he must use lighter weights and different types of exercise. All weight training should, of course, be under the supervision of a coach.

But the most important thing for a discus thrower to work on is his form in the circle. He must develop a smooth delivery of the discus or he will get no benefit from the spin. Discus throwers start working out in the fall, concentrating on form. During the winter, they can do sprint work to improve their speed and lift weights.

An athlete who combines the shot put and discus must work out a training program which will enable him to develop both skills. He should always work out with the heavier weight first to avoid possibility of muscle strains. Some time should be spent in the discus circle on almost every practice day in the spring.

The first skill a discus thrower must learn is how to hold the platter. The proper grip is shown in the picture below. The four fingers are comfortably spread, with the first joint hooked around the edge of the discus. The thumb rests on the back of the discus, as do the palm of the hand and the forearm.

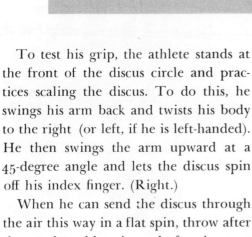

To test his grip, the athlete stands at the front of the discus circle and practices scaling the discus. To do this, he swings his arm back and twists his body to the right (or left, if he is left-handed). He then swings the arm upward at a 45-degree angle and lets the discus spin off his index finger. (Right.)

When he can send the discus through the air this way in a flat spin, throw after throw, the athlete is ready for the next step. He goes to the back of the circle and takes his stance, facing the front and swinging the discus back and forth in front of his body in the scaling motion.

As the arm swings back, he strides forward with the right leg, then with the left, twisting his body to the right on the second step. He then drives forward with the right leg, twisting the body to the left and bringing the arm up to release the discus.

This is called the "walking-in" style and can be used by beginners in competition while they are trying to master the spin. It is a good idea to take a couple of throws this way, get a satisfactory mark, and then try the spin. In this manner the athlete will be relaxed on the spin and will make more progress in perfecting it than if he has to worry about how far each throw goes.

This same strategy can be employed even after a discus thrower is using the spin on every throw. His first toss should be a relaxed, easy effort to get one mark to his credit. He will then find it easier to increase his speed on later throws without having to worry about a foul.

The Spin. — The object of the spin is to enable the athlete to release the discus at far greater velocity than with the standing or walk-in method. It must be a smooth, fast move and the arm, leg and body must be in proper position to work together on the throw.

The athlete goes into the spin (above). He has first taken several warmup swings across the body. The spin begins when the arm and hand reach the back point in the final swing.

Note the position of the feet, about eighteen inches apart, with toes facing the right side of the circle. The knees and hips are bent and the left arm is thrust out from the body to act as a balance. The two arms maintain these relative positions all the way through the spin.

The two mistakes to be avoided in the spin are: 1. to allow the throwing arm to catch up with the body so that it cannot deliver a full, sweeping motion at the end; 2. to allow the body to get too far in front of the arm so that its final twist to the left is completed before the arm starts its swing.

At upper right, the athlete has completed his full turn and is ready to come around for the throw. His right foot has made a full swing around the left from the original position and now the left is coming around to be planted for the throw. This swing of the right leg can be one circular hop. In neither case should the foot get more than six inches off the ground.

Proper distribution of weight throughout the spin will prevent the two mistakes mentioned previously. The weight of the body is on the right foot as the arm swings back to start the spin. It shifts to the left foot as the right leaves the ground and stays there while the right makes its full swing. The weight transfers back to the right foot when it completes the circle.

Notice that in the picture third from top the thrower's arm is still well in back of his body, but not too far back. The left arm is still extended for balance and both knees are slightly bent.

The athlete has planted the left foot and is coming up for the throw. The right arm has been carried through at a forty-five degree angle on the upswing, while the discus is released at near perfect timing with the direct forward facing of the body.

The follow-through at lower right shows good form and also the tremendous effort put into the throw as both feet of the thrower leave the ground after the release.

Former Olympic champion Sim Iness delivers a throw of over 184 feet. Notice the spread of his feet, in contrast to the picture on the previous page. Iness' feet are spread even more than the recommended three feet, his right arm is well back of the body and the right knee is bent. The whole force of his six-foot, five-inch frame is ready to get behind the sweep of the arm across the body. Iness might have been the first 200-foot discus thrower, had not illness cut short his career.

Another style of holding the discus (right). Instead of holding the palm and forearm flat against the platter, they are held slightly away from it. Since the discus is held entirely by the fingers, this is called the talon grip. It is used by some European athletes and allows the discus to leave the hand with less friction and thus a little more speed.

It is much harder to control the spin of the discus with the talon grip and only an athlete with large hands and very strong fingers can make sure that the discus will not slip out prematurely.

One of the most remarkable athletes of all time was Adolfo Consolini of Italy (left), who represented his country at four Olympic Games covering a period of twenty years.

He is shown here as his right foot comes around on the full swing. Note that both feet are off the ground at this point. The right will come around to land almost where the left is in this picture, and the left will swing around to be planted for the throw.

The development of the hop step in the discus is generally credited to Bob Fitch of Minnesota (right). It was further improved by another Minnesota athlete, Fortune Gordien, who held the world's record alternately with Consolini and Fitch over a period of fifteen years, 1941-1955.

Until Fitch and Gordien came along, most discus throwers concentrated on smoothness rather than speed in their spin. It was felt that a smooth delivery was more important than a fast one, for it insured that there would be no hitch in the motion to cause the arm, leg and body to lose their coordination.

One of the early stylists was 1932 Olympic champion, John Anderson (opposite). He is a picture of grace on his follow-through. He might almost be competing under the ancient Greek standard of form as well as distance.

Anderson's throw on this occasion was only 162 feet, 5 inches and this was only six feet better than the 1912 world's record, set when the circle was first extended from seven feet to its present size.

Fitch on the other hand, shows little style or grace as he goes through his warmup. His arm motion is not the usual one which brings the discus across the chest and, instead of being planted on both feet, his right leg is swinging back and forth.

But it took Fitch and Gordien to prove that the two-step swing of the right foot could be changed to a single hop. This turn in the air added to the speed of the thrower and also eliminated any chance of a hitch on that first step of the right foot.

These two athletes cut almost in half the time it took a thrower to cross the circle. This extra speed has enabled the world's record to be improved more than twenty feet since World War Two, whereas it improved only sixteen feet in the period from 1912 until 1946.

Women also throw the discus in competition, with their platter weighing two pounds, three and one fourth ounces. Nina Romaschkova of Russia sets an Olympic record of over 168 feet at the 1952 games at Helsinki (left). Her style is still not perfect for the right arm has gotten ahead of the right leg. Contrast this with Iness' form on page 154.

Women's competition has improved even more than men's since 1932. Lilian Copeland (right) of the United States is shown winning the 1932 Olympic title with a throw of 133 feet, 2 inches. She has not made the full move across the circle before releasing the discus and thus loses credit for several feet of her toss.

Here is former Olympic champion Gisele Mauermayer of Germany (left). She is using the old style of warmup with the arm coming down almost to knee level on the forward swing, instead of sweeping up to the chin. Her right foot is actually committing a foul as it rests on top of the rim of the circle. She faces the front of the circle, an unusual starting position.

Another great woman discus champion is Nina Ponomareva, right. Contrast this with the picture of Miss Mauermayer. Instead of an easy, relaxed warmup, here is a vigorous swing of body and arm. And instead of facing the front of the circle, the Russian champion faces directly backwards.

In contrast to the color picture on the opposite page this high school boy is shown from the rear as he is coiled and ready to begin his throw.

Javelin Throw

Spear-throwing contests among ancient warriors were the forerunner of the javelin throw. Though numbered among the weight events in track and field, it is quite different from the shot put, discus and hammer throws.

To begin with, the javelin is not thrown from a circle like the others. Instead, athletes are allowed an unlimited run to the scratch mark, though they must not pass this mark before, during or after the throw. The javelin is also much lighter than the other weight implements, weighing less than two pounds, though it is eight and a half feet long.

Javelin throwers generally are of slighter build than other weight men, though some are also shot-putters and discus throwers and therefore huskier than the average. The ideal build for the javelin is tall and wiry, with strong arm and leg muscles and a great throwing arm. The motion of the arm in tossing a javelin is a lot like that used to throw a baseball or a football.

High school, college and A.A.U. athletes use the same size javelin, another way in which this event differs from the shot and discus. A good high-school throw is over 170 feet, a great one is over 200 feet. In college and A.A.U. competition, 200 feet is rated fair, 225 feet is good and 250 feet or better is first class.

The chief problem in learning to throw the javelin is to coordinate the running approach with the delivery. Too many athletes run fast up to the scratch mark, then stop dead before they start the throw. They might just as well throw from a standing position for all the good the run does them. The secret lies in the footwork.

A javelin thrower must carefully measure his approach to the scratch mark, using the same system to do this as would a broad jumper in his event. He should allow for a run of about 100 feet, or 18 strides.

The three marks should be 18, 13 and five strides from the scratch mark. In the preliminary runs which establish these marks, the athlete must always carry the javelin and use the same approach he would for a throw. Otherwise, the marks would be useless.

There are several types of running approaches, but the most effective by far is the Finnish Front Cross-Step, named for the country in which it was developed. Beginners sometimes hop on the right leg to get the body turn necessary before the throw.

With the hop method, the final mark is only four strides from the scratch mark, instead of five. The athlete lands there with his right foot, hops and shifts his body to face to the right, then twists it back as he steps ahead with his left foot and brings the right arm up for the throw (for a right-handed thrower). For a left-hander, body and foot positions are reversed.

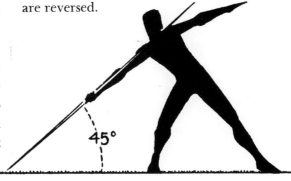

45°

Grip and Carry. — The proper handgrip of the javelin is shown below. The hand must hold the javelin by the cord grip, which is located at its center of gravity. The index finger curls around the wood behind the cord, while the middle finger and the thumb grip the back edge. An athlete should hold the javelin firmly but not tightly. The javelin is carried at shoulder level, with elbow bent.

The athlete (above) starts his running approach. His stride is that of a sprinter and the left arm is carried as in a dash. Perfect balance must be maintained through the run. A javelin thrower uses ordinary running spikes; under muddy conditions, football cleats are sometimes advisable and necessary.

The Cross-Step. — By the time he has passed the second mark, five strides from the start, the thrower should be traveling at nearly top speed. His object now is to maintain as much of that speed as possible until he releases the javelin. But he must also get his body in position for the throw, that is, twist it to the right side. The cross-step enables him to achieve both objectives.

At right, below, the thrower is about to plant his right foot at the final mark. His right arm has dropped down and back to get the javelin in position for the throw and his left arm has come forward to help maintain his balance. Notice that the right foot is pointing slightly to the side as it hits the ground.

At right is a perfect view of the cross-step. The left foot has taken its step forward and is planted pointing directly to the right side. The right leg swings by the left and the right arm is drawn all the way back for the throw.

The picture sequence on the preceding page took you through the carry, run and cross-step. On these two pages are rapid fire pictures completing the javelin throw, showing beautiful form in the ready position, body twist, release and follow through.

Study each picture from beginning to end carefully to detect the rhythm and fine overall body coordination attained by this thrower.

Above, the right foot has landed, toe pointing to the right. The left leg comes up to be planted facing forward. Just before the left foot lands, and while the athlete's weight is concentrated on his right leg, the arms begin the drive forward for the throw. The power comes from the right leg and, as the weight shifts to the left leg, is driven right through the twisting body to aid the arm and shoulder muscles.

The athlete (below) is ready to deliver the throw. The weight has now shifted over to the left leg and the body has completed its forward twist. It's all up to the arm now. The elbow leads the arm past the head and the javelin is held at a 45 degree angle. This enables the athlete to get maximum distance as he slings his forearm forward from the elbow and snaps his wrist to release the spear.

Some words of caution should be directed to potential javelin throwers. More arm injuries occur in this event than in all the other weight events combined. The arm and shoulder muscles must always be properly warmed up before throwing. Hard throwing in practice should be strictly limited; working on form should take up most of the practice time. Some champions throw for distance only in meets.

The javelin throw is one field event which has seen little improvement in technique since the Finns developed the cross-step in the 1920s. Rather, it has been the implement itself which has been improved so that it sails more easily through the air, enabling athletes to get extra distance on their throws.

But there has been a vast improvement in American javelin throwing since the end of World War Two. For the first time, U. S. athletes compete on even terms with the Scandinavian stars. The pictures (below and upper right) show how American technique has changed.

A javelin thrower of the late 1930s is about to let the spear go (below). Notice that his left foot has already hit the

ground before he has started the arm swing upward. This means that a good part of his weight has also shifted to that foot and will not be behind the throw. It also means that the left foot will act as a brake on the speed he has built up down the runway and further shorten his throw.

The athlete who popularized the Finnish style of throwing in the United States, Dr. Steve Seymour (right, above). His left foot has also hit the ground, but he is already far enough through the throw so that the shift of weight to the left foot is natural and does not affect the natural flow of power to the arm.

Notice the extreme bend of the elbow as the arm comes through the air. The delivery will be almost like a whip with the elbow and wrist both "cracking" to send the spear zooming into space.

In almost the same position is Egil Danielsen of Norway (lower right) as he sets a world's record of 281 feet, 2¼ inches while winning the 1956 Olympic title at Melbourne. Each part of his body — feet, legs, trunk, arms and head — is in almost the same position as Seymour. If there is one difference, it is that Danielsen's trunk is more erect, while Seymour bends slightly to the left.

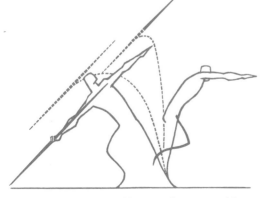

Arm and body working together as a whip.

A thrower uses a three-quarter over-hand delivery (right), which is typical of athletes who also compete in the shot put and discus. Their bulky upper arm development makes the straight over-hand delivery almost impossible. For this reason, champion javelin throwers rarely compete in other events after college days.

The smallest of the javelin champions, is shown below. Al Cantello, who broke Danielsen's world record in 1959, is only five feet, eight. He has developed his own style of follow-through. He leaves the ground as he lets go of the spear and follows it through the air, landing on his chest, just short of the scratch line. He believes it compensates for his lack of height.

A side view (left) of Seymour getting off his American record throw of 248 feet, 10 inches, in 1947. It was this throw that placed American javelin throwers into the world picture. Notice the great strain of the leg muscles at the moment of delivery. Also note the perfect 45-degree angle of the javelin, a split-second after it has left his hand.

The greatest American thrower before Seymour was Bob Peoples, shown in a follow-through (right). His right leg comes up to the scratch line as the left leg goes back. This allows him to land in a perfectly balanced position with no danger of crossing the line and committing a foul.

The women's javelin is slightly shorter and lighter than the men's javelin. Above, Karen Anderson, an American javelin thrower, is shown ready to make a throw while competing in the 1956 Olympics at Royal Park, Victoria, Australia. Karen is the holder of several javelin throwing records in the United States.

Showing graceful form as she nears the point of release is Tilly Fleischer, former woman Olympic champion javelin thrower from Germany.

Hammer Throw

The most specialized of all track and field events is the hammer throw. Competition in the United States is limited strictly to New England in high school and to the eastern coast in college. Athletes in this event enjoy long competitive careers, and it is not unusual to see a hammer thrower still active at the age of forty-five.

Closely allied to the hammer throw are the two heavy weight throws, the 35-pound in indoor competition and the 56-pound in outdoor competition. Hammer and weight throwers are large, husky men, most of them over six feet tall and well over two hundred pounds.

The hammer is a 12-pound (high-school) or 16-pound (college and A.A.U.) iron ball attached by wire to a triangular metal grip. The thrower holds the grip with the second joint of the fingers of his left hand and wraps the right hand over the left. A glove is usually worn on the left hand. (Southpaw throwers should reverse the grip, with the right hand on the grip and the left over it.)

No one should attempt to learn how to throw the hammer without expert coaching. Except in New England, few Americans touch a hammer until they enter college. Practice and competition in this event must be held in an area where the spectators and other athletes are shielded by a cage or net from a wild throw. The hammer is thrown from a seven-foot circle, usually painted on a hard rock surface.

Hammer throwing technique was brought to a high level long before that of most other track and field events. In the early 1900s a group of Irish-American athletes dominated the event and achieved distances of over 170 feet, in some cases of over 180 feet. These are still creditable marks.

High-school athletes, with their lighter hammer, usually throw between 170 and 190 feet in championship meets. College throwers do well to hit 180 feet, though some of the best have surpassed 200 feet. On the international level, marks over 210 feet are not uncommon. Eastern Europeans, including Russians and Scandinavians, usually provide the chief competition for Americans in this event at the Olympic Games.

The trick in throwing the hammer is to be able to turn three times in the circle and release the weapon without having the momentum of the throw carry you out of the circle for a foul. Beginners throw with one turn, then increase to two and finally to three. It was the introduction of the third turn, plus the change to hard-surface circles, which enabled modern athletes to pass the 200-foot mark in this event.

Long arms are a necessary physical characteristic for the hammer thrower. The farther away from the body that the hammer swings in the turns across the circle, the longer it will go in flight. It takes several years to develop good form in this event, but once an athlete develops a "groove" of throwing, he seldom loses it. Some veteran throwers never touch a hammer between meets.

A hammer thrower is pictured (opposite) as he swings across the circle. Notice the full extension of his arms, elbows perfectly straight. The pivot for the turn is being made on the outside of his left foot, which should not leave the ground during the turn. On each turn, the athlete advances about two feet across the circle so that he is at the front when he lets the hammer go.

The path of the hammer during the turns is a circle angled 45 degrees from the ground. The hammer travels up on the left side of the body and down on the right side (for a right-handed thrower). It reaches its lowest point, six inches from the ground, when it is just off his right heel. The high point is reached when the hammer is over his left shoulder, the point at which it will be finally released.

Getting a firm grip on the hammer, the athlete steps into the circle facing toward the back. He then takes several preliminary swings, without moving his feet, which are about twenty inches apart. These swings carry the hammer through the same path as just outlined for the turn, but with the difference that the elbows must bend to bring the hammer over his head.

To hold proper balance the body must be erect, but with the weight slightly forward and chiefly on the left leg. The weight will stay on that leg all the way across the circle, to provide a brake for the body. Otherwise, the force of the swinging hammer can carry the athlete right off his feet.

The pivot on the left foot starts from the outside of the heel and moves along the side of the foot to the outside of the

toes as the turn is completed. The right foot stays on the ground as long as it can after the hammer starts its swing, then makes a quick circular move — up, around and down. This footwork is repeated for each turn.

Unlike the shot, discus and javelin, the hammer must get in front of the body during the approach to the throw — otherwise the athlete will fall flat on his face. For with both arms busy swinging the hammer, it is the iron ball itself which helps to balance the body while the right foot is off the ground. The hammer leads the body as it starts its swing up to the left; is even when the right foot reaches its highest point halfway through the circular step; then gets behind the body for the downswing as the right foot completes its step.

In order for the hammer to get out in front again for the second turn, the thrower must slow his motion after the right foot hits the ground. This allows the hammer to swing around and up and lead him into the second turn.

This second turn is slightly faster than the first. The athlete must be careful, as his speed increases, to keep both arms fully extended at all times and to control the arc of the hammer so that it follows the sharp up-and-down path and does not merely circle his waist.

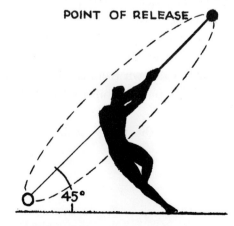

POINT OF RELEASE

45°

Al Hall, (above) a 200-foot thrower, is shown as he swings his right leg around on the third turn. Notice that his pivot is being made on the side of his foot and that the hammer is even with his body as it comes over the right shoulder. His right knee is tightly bent and the foot kept high so that it will not hit the ground prematurely. His pivot has shifted to the outside of the toes (right) and the vigorous step of his right leg is now bringing his body in front of the hammer.

Hall is ready to plant his right foot, but he has erred in letting his left foot leave the ground. This will put his body at the mercy of the hammer and he will not be able to control the path of its swing on the final swoop down before the release. Actually his weight at this point should be more concentrated on the left foot than on the earlier turns, for it must provide a firm pivot around which both arms and the rest of the body will swing to release the hammer.

Now we see what has happened as a result of that error in the third picture. The hammer has come around much too high and will not reach a 45-degree arc for the takeoff. It is also too far in front of the body for Hall to get the full benefit of his legs and twisting trunk behind it. Still, the momentum of the turns insures a good throw, in this case over 180 feet. Another problem resulting from the one mistake is that the hammer has carried Hall dangerously close to the outside rim of the circle.

The hammer swings up to be released. In an effort to prevent a foul, Hall has brought his right foot behind his left leg, for the normal forward step of the right leg at this point would take him over the line. At far right, he has let the hammer go, but his arms, instead of being high over his head, are extended straight forward. The proper form for the release is to bring the hammer up from the ground, arms traveling almost vertically with the ball being released over the left shoulder, instead of halfway between chest and shoulder, as in this instance.

Harold Connolly (right), 1956 Olympic champion, starts his swing for a throw. Connolly was the first American to throw over 200 feet and the first athlete in the world to reach 225 feet. He accomplished these feats despite a handicapped left arm. His success is another testimonial to the pluck and fortitude of track and field champions.

The proper form in the circle before beginning the turns is shown (left). This athlete is swinging the hammer around his head, just before he starts the first turn. His feet are set comfortably about two feet apart and he faces the back of the circle. This picture was taken when dirt circles were used, rather than the concrete one from which Connolly is throwing.

A great thrower of yesterday, Bernie Healion of Ireland, is shown (left) as he brings the hammer up and around on his final turn. A left-hander, Healion has his inside grip on the hammer with his right hand. He pivots on his right foot and will release the hammer over his right shoulder.

This Japanese athlete (right) has just released the hammer. His right foot starts up to join the left at the front of the circle and provide balance so that he does not follow the hammer out of the circle. Note the lines on the ground at right and left marking the 90-degree sector in which the hammer must fall.

179

Cross-Country

Cross-country running demands endurance, the ability to run in any kind of weather and the love of competing for the pure sake of the sport itself.

The cross-country season in the United States begins in late September and closes in early December. It is actually not much more than a training period for the indoor and outdoor seasons which are to follow.

The races are run over hilly courses in open country, rather than on a cinder track. The usual distance for a high school race is 1.8 or two and a half miles, for a college race four or five miles, and an A.A.U. race six miles, or 10,000 meters.

Because of the nature of a cross-country course and because of the weather at that season of the year, special equipment is required. Cross-country shoes have soft rubber heels and come with or without spikes, as some courses are run partly on hard surfaces. Runners wear light gloves and soft wool leggings when they have to run in extremely cold weather.

Since cross-country is actually distance running on a hill and dale course, athletes employ the same style of running and the same training methods as in the distance events we have already discussed. But there are a few added tricks.

When running uphill, the athlete must shorten his stride, bring his knees higher and swing his arms upward. This gives the added strength necessary to carry him up the hills, many of which are extremely steep.

Coming downhill, the runner should "let himself go," coasting to take advantage of the terrain. But he must keep an eye out for pitfalls on the ground, especially on a strange course. When he hits the flat again, he should allow his momentum to carry him along until he is back traveling at his regular pace.

A cross-country race should be run at a fairly even pace until the final 440 yards when the runner can increase his speed, still saving something for the final burst to the tape. On strange courses, it is wise to follow a member of the home team, otherwise there is the chance of being lost.

Since cross-country is a team sport, it is good policy to train members of the same team to run together in pairs or threesomes over at least the first three-quarters of the course. This way, there is less chance of one of the boys falling back and adding unnecessary points to the score.

Whatever your specialty in track and field, cross-country running in the fall can be of value to you. It strengthens the leg muscles and generally puts your body in top physical condition. Indeed, European athletes treat it almost entirely as a conditioner, running very few races.

The picture above shows a section of the starting line of the four mile run during the Fifth Annual N.A.I.A. Cross Country Championship held at Omaha, Nebraska in November 1960.

The caliber of cross country running among N.A.I.A. schools is showing marked improvement. The 1960 meet started 87 runners and 83 finished, representing nineteen schools from ten states. The overall times were faster than previous years with a new course record being set by Joe Thomas of Southern Illinois, timed at 20:39 to lower the previous record of 20:55.6.

Southern Illinois also set a team scoring record of 37 points. The old low total of 45 was set by Howard Payne in 1957.

The leaders at about the two mile post (opposite above), are Odvaar Helgeson, North Dakota State, in first place with the eventual winner Joe Thomas right on his heels. In third place is Earl Detrick of Graceland College who came in second at the finish. Helgeson finished in fourth position.

Joe Thomas is seen crossing the finish line (right) well ahead of the pack as the timer at his left is ready to clock his new record time.

Three beautiful views on these two pages show the Third National Collegiate Athletic Association (N.C.A.A.) College Division Cross Country Championships held at Wheaton College, Wheaton, Illinois during the fall of 1960. One hundred and thirty-seven athletes participated, representing twenty-one colleges.

The start (below) shows all 137 runners reacting to the gun.

The pack is strung out (right) as the runners approach the three-quarter mile mark.

After two miles (lower right) seven runners in a tight group have moved well out in front of the rest of the field.

A Series of Workouts for Cross Country

The following 8 items may be used as a basis for individual workouts and are to be used on the running track. However, if a mile or the required distance can be laid out on grass, some of the workouts should be done there.

1. Warm-up calisthenics
   20 minutes easy running
   Rest by walking 10 minutes
   Run a 440 at 1¼ of your 440 time
   Jog 10 minutes to cool off

2. Warm-up calisthenics
   Two individual miles at 6 minutes, rest by walking between each for 10 minutes.
   Rest by walking 10 minutes
   Run an 880 at 1¼ of your 880 time
   Rest by walking 5 minutes
   Run a 440 at 70 seconds
   Jog 10 minutes to cool off

3. Warm-up calisthenics
   Run 4 miles at an easy jog
   Walk 10 minutes
   Run a 440 at 70 seconds
   Jog 10 minutes to cool off

4. Warm-up calisthenics
   Run a mile in 5:15
   Rest by walking 10 minutes
   Run a mile in 5:15
   Rest by walking 10 minutes

Run an 880 at 1¼ of your 880 time
Jog 10 minutes to cool off

5. Warm-up calisthenics
   Run four 660's at 1:50, jog a 440 between each
   Walk 10 minutes
   Run four 150 yard wind sprints, jogging 150 yards between each
   Walk 5 minutes
   Jog 10 minutes to cool off

6. Warm-up calisthenics
   Run 3 miles at 20 minutes
   Rest by walking 10 minutes
   Run a mile at an easy jog
   Rest by walking 5 minutes
   Jog 10 minutes to cool off

7. Warm-up calisthenics
   Run eight 440's at 75, jogging a lap between each
   Rest by walking 10 minutes
   Jog 10 minutes to cool off

8. Warm-up calisthenics
   Up and down the ladder
   Run a 440 in 70 seconds
   Jog a lap
   Run a 660 in 1:50
   Jog a lap
   Run a 880 in 2:35
   Jog a lap
   Run a 660 in 1:50
   Jog a lap
   Run a 440 in 70 seconds
   Rest by walking 10 minutes
   Jog an easy mile to cool off

Cross Country Workouts on a Daily Basis

MONDAY. — Long, easy, over distance running on grass. Terrain to hilly, rolling with some flat surfaces. A golf course is ideal, or a park.

TUESDAY. — On the track a series of 440's run at a pace of between 70 to 75 seconds. The number will vary with each boy. Early in the year four quarters jogging a 440 between each. At the end of this, rest by walking an 880, and then build up 880 by starting out slow and gradually building up speed finishing the last 150 yards wide open.

WEDNESDAY. — Running at a park or golf course where a given distance of 660 or an 880 can be laid out is suggested for this day. A 660 in 115 seconds with the 880 in 2:35 is a good time. Four to five of these with the same distance being jogged between each is enough — try to hit the time exactly.

THURSDAY. — A mile on the track at a good fast pace is sufficient. Over distance jogging of approximately two miles to cool off.

FRIDAY. — A rest day if before a meet on Saturday, however, early in the season this can be used for specific pace work over short distances of 440, 550 or 660.

Ted Nelson, former Mankato State College star held the N.A.I.A. 880 record for three years (1958-1960) with a time of 1:51.8.

Know Your Sport

What are the events in track and field championship programs?

100-yard dash, 220-yard dash, 440-yard run, 880-yard run, mile, three-mile run, six-mile run, two-mile walk, 120-yard high hurdles, 220-yard low hurdles, 440-yard hurdles, two-mile steeplechase, running high jump, pole vault, running broad jump, running hop, step and jump, 16 lb. shot put, discus throw, javelin throw, 16 lb. hammer throw and 56 lb. weight throw.

How long in distance is the marathon?
26 miles, 385 yards.

How many officials are required for an outdoor track and field championship meet?

59, including one referee, one starter, seven finish judges, five inspectors, five timers, three clerks, one walking judge, 24 field judges, three marshals, one scorer, one announcer, one doctor, one surveyor, one recorder of records, one press steward, one inspector of implements, one custodian of numbers and prizes and one photo-finish clerk.

Which official makes decisions on all questions relating to the games and makes the final settlement on matters not otherwise assigned by the rules?

The referee.

A racer leading the field in a 100-yard dash nears the finish line and thrusts his arms forward across the line. Does the timer record the time at the instant the sprinter's arm crosses the line?

No. The rules state that "the time shall be taken from the flash of the pistol to the moment at which any part of the competitor's body (i.e., the "torso," as distinguished from the head, arms, hands, legs or feet, but including the neck) reaches the nearest edge of the finish line."

A track star is pacing the pack as he nears the finish line with his nearest pursuer five yards back. As he approaches the line he stumbles and falls, the upper half of his body crossing the line. While he is lying on the ground, his pursuer crosses the line. Who wins the race?

The pursuer. The rules state "a competitor falling at the finish is not considered to have finished unless his entire body shall have crossed the finish line.

A miler breezes across the finish line far ahead of his competitors, but there is disagreement among the timers whose watches disagree. The first watch registered 4:10.6. The second showed 4:11 and the third said 4:10.4. What is the official time of the race?

4:10.6. The time shown by the watch recording the middle time shall be the official time if all three watches disagree.

This same miler wins his next mile outing but, unfortunately, there is another mix-up among the timers. The first timer's watch shows 4:09.8. The second shows 4:11. The third watch didn't register at all. What is the official time of the race?

4:11. If for any reason only two watches record the time of the event and they fail to agree, the longer time of the two shall be accepted as the official time.

A walking judge sees a contestant walking unfairly and warns him about the infraction. A hundred steps later the judge again notices the competitor making the same violation. What happens then?

The walking judge immediately upon the second warning disqualifies the competitor.

A walker who has not been warned at all during the race is leading by a few strides as he nears the finish line. About 100 meters away from the finish the walking judge notices an infraction. What does the judge do?

He disqualifies the competitor even though it was his first warning because the rule states the judge "shall immediately disqualify any competitor when walking unfairly during the last 200 meters of a race.

How long is a meter?

39.37 inches.

The 100-yard dash is about to begin and an over-eager sprinter beats the gun. Three others follow, jumping the gun also. The starter is required to warn the offender and then disqualify the offender if it happens a second time. How many sprinters does the starter warn?

Only one. The rules are quite specific in this matter. When a competitor beats the gun "others are inclined to follow and strictly speaking, any competitor who does so follow, has beaten the gun. The starter should warn only such competitor or competitors who in his opinion were responsible for beating the gun."

Which is the true mark of finish, the finish line drawn on the ground or the tape extended across the track?

The line drawn on the ground is the official finish. The tape is there for the purpose of aiding the judges.

In races on tracks of one or more turns how far does one runner have to be ahead of a competitor before he crosses in front of him?

Two yards.

A hillbilly enters high school and proves to be a natural sprinter, but unfortunately he doesn't wear shoes. His teammates get him to get used to shoes which would give him a firmer grip on the ground than he would have in bare feet. The hillbilly agrees but just before the start of the race he decides against it. So he compromises by taking off one shoe and leaving the other on. He races and wins. Is he given credit officially as the winner?

Yes. The rules state a competitor may compete in bare feet or with footwear on one or both feet.

A pole vaulter arrives late at the meet and finds that the pole vaulting is already in progress and the bar is at 13 feet. Since the boy always started at 12 feet, 6 inches and moved up from there, he asks the officials to lower the bar for him. Will they honor his request?

No. The bar will not be lowered for any contestant reporting late.

Is it permissible for a pole vaulter to use resin on his hands to get a better grip on the pole?

Yes.

A pole vaulter has difficulty seeing the crossbar because of the hazy sky in the background. To ease this difficulty he takes his handkerchief and places it on the crossbar so he can estimate his jump more accurately. Does the official allow him to do this or does he tell him to put his handkerchief back in his pocket?

He allows him to leave the handkerchief on the crossbar. The rules state the competitor "may place a handkerchief on the crossbar for sighting purposes."

The rule states that the competitor must take off from one foot.

A powerful javelin thrower unleashes a strong heave. While in flight, the javelin breaks in two, the front half setting a new record and the rear falling to the ground five feet short. What is the ruling?

It doesn't count as an official toss if the javelin breaks while in the air, the rule states.

In the 120-yard hurdles how far from the start is the first hurdle?

15 yards.

In a handicap medley race is the longest distance run first or last?

It is run first.

A track and field meet is held outdoors under a threatening sky. The first pole vaulter sets a new record. As the second competitor prepares to try it begins to rain very hard. After waiting vainly for

A high jumper has developed a novel technique in secret practice and it is quite successful, he leaps from both feet and with amazing results. Then he tried it out on his coach, who marvelled at his jumps but told him to forget about that style. Why?

the rain to stop the referee postpones the event. What happens to the record?

It doesn't count. The rule says that any postponed event which was already in progress shall be conducted "at a future date in the same manner as though the competition had never been started."

Ron Drummond, discus thrower, is being judged and scored by the panel of men to his left during a meet in California.

Scoring a Meet

Team championship in United States track and field outdoor competition is determined under Amateur Athletic Union rules on the basis of 10 points for each first place scored; 8 points for second; 6 points for third; 4 points for fourth; 2 points for fifth, and 1 point for sixth.

District Association championships and point trophies for other outdoor meets sanctioned by any district association may be scored on a 5-3-2-1 point basis for the first four places.

All indoor meets, whether for the U.S. championships or any District Association-sanctioned meet, shall be scored on the 5-3-2-1 system for the first four places.

This scoring applies to all events both in the track and the field competition.

Scoring in the cross-country race requires special attention. Not more than seven men may start for any team and only the first five members of each to finish "count" on team scoring. Other runners, the 6th and 7th men, are used as pushers.

The total of the positions of the first five members of each team is that team's point score and the team with the lowest total points is the winner. For instance, if Team A's five men finish in 1st, 4th, 5th, 8th and its fifth man tied for 9th and 10th positions, its score would be 27½, the sum of the five runners' finishing spots.

If Team B's five winners finished 2nd, 3rd, 6th, 7th and its fifth man tied for 9th and 10th, its total would also be 27½, tying it with Team A.

The sixth and seventh men for each team are also very valuable in as much as they often force another team's man or men to finish farther back; ie: In a team meet, team A has spots 1-3-5-10-11-14 and 15; team B has 2-4-12-13 and 17; team C has 6-7-8-9 and 16; team A is the winner with its first five men totaling 30 points, team C with 46 points is second and Team B is third with 48 points. In this case team A's sixth and seventh men forced C's fifth man to be 16th and B's fifth man to come in 17th.

The marathon is run virtually the same way with a few changes. For example, not more than six men may start for any one team and only the first three members of any team to finish count in the scoring. Otherwise the team whose finishing figures add up to the lowest total is the winner, just as in the cross-country competition.

If, in either the cross-country or marathon, two competitors finish in a tie the sum total of the finishing positions is divided between the two runners. For instance, if two men tied for second, they would each get 2½ points, representing the total of the finishing position (2nd and 3rd adding up to 5, divided by two).

If the final over-all scoring of the meet shows two teams with even scores, the championship is given to the team scoring the most first places.

If the tie still remains after this counting, the tying teams are designated co-champions.

Growth of Track and Field

THE TRACK AND FIELD movement in America began in 1876, an even dozen years after the first official meet in England between Oxford and Cambridge.

Two great athletic associations, the Amateur Athletic Union of America and the Intercollegiate Association of Amateur Athletes of America, held their first championship contests in 1876 and have conducted them annually since then.

The spirit of '76 was contagious and track and field blossomed all over America, especially in the eastern half. But its operation was not the smoothly-run setup it is today. People were running and jumping, but there was little order in the overall operation.

In 1888 the National Amateur Athletic Union was founded. This came at a time when you couldn't tell the amateurs from the professionals without a scorecard and athletics was in the hands of shady promoters. Since that time the NAAU has run amateur track and field with an iron hand insuring fairness and honesty to both athletes and fans alike.

Members of the New York Athletic Club, the first such organization in this country, get ready to take off on a 100-yard dash.

Another milestone was the inception of high school competition. The first scholastic meet was conducted by the University of Pennsylvania in 1895.

The following year America was able to field a fine team to represent it at the resumption of the Olympic Games in Athens, winning nine out of twelve events.

Interstate high school competition began at the University of Chicago Interscholastic Meet in 1901. These games were run under the direction of Amos Alonzo Stagg, the famous football coach.

In 1905 the National Collegiate Athletic Association was organized and staged its first track and field championship in 1921.

The year before, the National Federation of State High School Athletic Associations was formed to standardize rules and regulations for high school athletics.

These various organizations, working separately and with one another, formed the solid foundation on which American athletics is based.

Early American Athletes. — The very first American champion was a gentleman named I. Frazer of the Yonkers Lyceum. Frazer was a broad jumper and the AAU recorded his winning leap at 17 feet, 4 inches. This mark seems rather puny when compared to the modern day record of 26 feet, 8¼ inches established by Olympic great Jesse Owens in 1935, but Frazer's leap set the standards of the day and the youthful broad jumpers set about to break his mark, which they did quite regularly.

One sure way of precipitating an argument is to compare the greats of today with the old-timers of yesteryear. Can the record-shattering performance of the moderns be attributed simply to greater natural ability?

Most authorities doubt this and offer several reasons why new records are set with almost clock-like regularity and why many of the modern marks are so far superior to those set by champions of the past.

One reason advanced is that increased interest in the events has encouraged far more athletes to compete, thus inspiring greater efforts.

Another is that the human desire for improved performance has spurred the individual athlete on to study his own individual strong and weak points and get the most out of his own personal physical equipment.

Thirdly, there have been improved techniques developed by astute coaches and applied to brilliant athletes. One of the first of the radical coaching improvements was made by Mike Murphy, the famous coach of the University of Pennsylvania. Murphy developed the crouch start for the sprint.

In the late 1890s Murphy had a sprinter named Sherrill whom he taught the crouch. When Sherrill first introduced it in a race the official called time thinking that Sherrill didn't know the proper way to start, which, at the time, was from a standing position.

After he explained, Sherrill was allowed to adopt his novel technique. He won handily, aided by the early advantage received at the start, and from then on the stand-up start for the sprints faded rapidly.

Another reason to take in mind when comparing modern and old-time records is that today's average youngster is bigger and stronger than his counterpart of fifty or sixty years ago. This is undoubtedly a factor in any contests based on speed, strength and endurance.

Hurdles of the 1880s stretched right across the track. When a hurdle was knocked over, so was the race.

A perfect example of how records have shot skyward is illustrated in the history of the high jump. The first record was set by H. E. Ficken of the New York Athletic Club, who leaped 5 feet, 5 inches. Interest in competitive jumping soared and countless youths began learning how to jump. Just sixteen years later, in 1892, Michael F. Sweeney added almost a foot to Ficken's record by clearing 6 feet, 4½ inches. Three years later he added another inch and one-eighth. Higher and higher the record climbed and sports experts began to envision a human who could top seven feet. And eventually that

"ceiling" was reached and passed. Y. Stepanov of Russia jumped 7 feet, 1 inch in 1957.

Another illustration lies in the development of pole vaulting. The Greek word for the sport is translated as "spear high jump," while the German word "Stabhochsprung" means "staff high jump."

From the Greek word it can be seen that pole vaulting was a military device, with the soldiers using their spears to clear obstacles as they strove to attack the enemy or flee from them. The German word goes back to the days when young-

Cornelius Warmerdam became the first man ever to clear 15 feet in the pole vault. Connie did it not once, but 43 times before he closed out a fabulous career. He got as high as 15 feet, 7½ inches.

sters tended their flocks of sheep using a staff to guide the animals. Undoubtedly the staffs were used as an aid to jump stone fences or other barriers.

As was noted earlier, pole vaulting was at first a horizontal leap. Later it was changed to a height contest and in 1877 it was added to the list of events in America. The first American to hold a record was G. McNichol, who registered 9 feet, 7 inches in 1877.

Through the years the mark rose higher. The maximum height that man could reach was 15 feet, the experts said, as the vaulters set about to reach that figure. Finally Cornelius Warmerdam came along. He shattered all theories about man's capabilities in pole vaulting. He topped 15 feet not once, not twice, but 43 times during his brilliant career. His highest flight was registered at 15 feet, 7½ inches. But even that magnificent achievement didn't remain a record very long. In 1957, R. A. Gutowski padded down the runway at Palo Alto, California, and when he came to rest in the pit he had cleared the bar at a fantastic 15 feet, 8¼ inches.

Shot-putting came from an ancient pastime practiced in Scotland and Ireland, called putting the stone. The stone weighed 14 pounds and was block-shaped with rounded edges. Even today in British countries the stone is considered a unit of weight. For instance, a 210-pound heavyweight would be said to weigh 15 stone under British weights, figuring it at 14 pounds per stone.

The event was on the first AAU program in 1876 and the winner was H. E.

Buermeyer of the New York Athletic Club with a toss of 32 feet, 5 inches. In 1909 Ralph Rose of the Olympic Club reached 51 feet. Jim Fuchs, Yale's great star, put the shot 58 feet, 10¾ inches in 1950. Then along came Parry O'Brien who set the present-day mark in 1956 with a heave of 63 feet, 2 inches.

Early records in track competition were much closer to today's standards than the first marks in field events. The 100-yard dash is a perfect illustration.

In the 100 there were no wholesale marks set as noted in the field events. This was because the first record was a real problem to beat. It was made by John Owen, who did the 100 in 9.8 at Washington, D. C., in 1890. Twelve years later, Arthur Duffey, standing 5 foot, 7 inches and weighing a wiry 138 pounds, breezed home in 9.6.

Later, Bob Gutowski came along to snap Warmerdam's record with a flight of 15 feet, 8¼ inches.

Two of the greatest of all sprinters, Bobby Morrow, left, and Dave Sime battle for the tape, first reached by Morrow.

This mark withstood the onslaughts of many great runners, including Charley Paddock, the "world's fastest human." Charley tied the mark six times but never broke it officially. However, judges agreed that Charley had several times done the 100 in 9.5, but in those days the watches recorded only fifth-second times as opposed to the tenth-second timing done today. Even though he had flashed to the wire in 9.5 he could not be given credit for it officially and had to be content with tying the mark at 9.6.

Finally Frank Wykoff of the University of Southern California made 9.4 in 1930. The mark was tied by Jesse Owens in 1935.

Thirteen years later, a speedster named Mel Patton chopped a decisive tenth-of-

a-second and set a 9.3 mark. By this time the timing watches which record tenths-of-seconds were in use.

Since Patton's dash, his mark was tied eight times by five different racers, with Dave Sime of Duke equalling the record on three occasions.

Frank Budd of Villanova finally broke Patton's mark when he registered a time of 9.2 seconds during the N.C.A.A. meet at Villanova in June 1961.

One of the outstanding early-day American athletes was a thin youngster named Lawrence (Lon) Myers. This versatile speedster stood 5 feet, 8 inches tall and weighed only 114 pounds. No one could figure out where he got the endurance one day in 1880 when he competed in seven races in a single afternoon and won four American championships in the 100, 220, 440 and 880.

Myers was a fellow who wanted to win and never bothered himself too much about setting records. Even so, he held the national record for the 440, doing it in 48.6, in 1881.

This mark stood for five years when it was cracked by Wendell Baker of Harvard, who lost a shoe, but gained a record. About halfway from the finish line Baker developed a sore foot. Apparently a cut had opened and it began to bleed. Without breaking stride, Baker kicked off his shoe and romped home for a new record. His official time was 47.6.

The best mark in the first sixty years of this century was 45.7, set in 1958 by Glenn Davis of Ohio State University, winner of that year's James E. Sullivan

No hurdler ever came close to the marks established by Glenn Davis of Ohio State.

A.A.U. Memorial Award. Davis edged Rafer Johnson, world decathlon champion from the University of California at Los Angeles (U.C.L.A.) in the closest voting race in the history of the award.

Hurdling is a comparatively recent addition to the track and field program. There were no hurdles in ancient Greece nor in the legends of any other country. They go back only to the early 19th century in England. They were held at Eton and the first record was set by A. W. T. Daniel, who did the 120 high hurdles in 17¾ seconds in 1864.

The University of Pennsylvania, long a spawning ground for track and field stars, produced the man considered to be the father of modern hurdling, Alvin Kraenzlein. In 1898 Kraenzlein held the American record with a mark of 23.6. The best mark through 1959 was 22.1, set by Elias Gilbert on May 17, 1958. So, in more than sixty years, the time for the 220-yard hurdles has been reduced only one-and-one-half seconds.

Relay racing is a newcomer to athletic programs, having been made a part of the games only in 1893. Frank B. Ellis and H. L. Geyelin were the "inventors" of the four-man race. They introduced it that year in the Pennsylvania Relays in order to make the games more interesting. How successful their innovation was is attested to by the fact that nearly every high school and college track team has a relay racing unit.

The Encyclopedia Britannica gives credit to the Massachusetts Firemen's "bean-pot" race as being the forerunner of modern relay racing:

Rafer Johnson, who held the decathlon record going into the 1960s, was an all-round athlete at University of California at Los Angeles.

"The old method was for the men running the second quarter of the race each to take over a small flag from the first relay men as they arrived, before departing on their own stage of the race, at the end of which they, in turn, handed on their flags to the awaiting runners. The flags, however, were considered cumbersome and for a time it was sufficient for the outgoing runner to touch or be touched by his predecessor."

The discus throw is the oldest event in field competition. Homer mentions throwing the quoit (discus) in the games held at the funeral of Patroclus and it was a standard part of the pentathlon during the Olympics of long ago.

M. J. Sheridan in 1808 set the discus record with a throw of 134 feet, 2 inches. The discus throw is a field event which shows a rapid rate of record-breaking down through the years. The best mark through 1959 was by Fortune Gordien, who threw the discus 194 feet, 6 inches in a meet at Pasadena, California in 1953.

The javelin throw was used by the mighty German warrior, Siegfried, to display his strength and athletic ability. King Henry VIII of England was reportedly quite handy with the javelin, but unlike the Greek King Œnomaus, who killed trouble-makers and potential sons-in-law with a javelin, Henry threw the javelin for pleasure. Whenever he wanted to dispose of some person who irritated him, he resorted to the guillotine. It was handy and it didn't require half the energy of throwing a javelin.

Competitive javelin throwing records have become almost an exclusive Scan-

One of the all-time discus greats is Fortune Gordien, who spun the platter for the University of Minnesota.

Egil Danielsen of Norway wheeled the javelin 281 feet, 2¼ inches for a new record in the 1956 Olympics.

is 54 feet, 5 inches and it was set by a Russian athlete, O. Rjakhovsky, in 1958.

The half-mile, or 880-yard race, has been more or less the step-child of racing coming as it does in the shadow of its more renowned brother, the mile race.

Lon Myers, the stringbean racer in the 1880s who concentrated only on winning, held the half-mile mark gliding across in 1:55.4 way back in 1886. Tom Courtney's 1:46.8, accomplished in 1957, was the best in sixty years.

dinavian property. From the first records to the present day the leading spear throwers were rugged souls from the cold country. Eric Lemming of Sweden held the first mark in 1906 with a toss of 175 feet, 6 inches. A Finn named Yrjo Nikkanen held the crown in 1938 with a record heave of 258 feet, 2⅜ inches. Then along came a Norwegian, Egil Danielson, who astounded spectators at the 1956 Olympic games in Melbourne, Australia, by throwing the javelin 281 feet, 2 inches.

The first hop-step-jump record in the United States was held by Dan Ahearne, who covered 50 feet, 11 inches in 1911. Today's record isn't too much higher. It

The world's fastest half-miler of the first sixty years of this century was Tom Courtney, the flash from Fordham.

Assault on the Mile. — The mile race, today the biggest attraction on nearly every card, was just another event up until the mid-1920s, playing second fiddle to the 100-yard dash and several other contests. Then a runner came along who excited the world with a sparkling display of endurance and speed that placed new importance on the mile run. The man was Paavo Nurmi, the Flying Finn, who galloped out of the forests of Finland to become one of the greatest names in the history of athletics. He wasn't the first great miler. In fact, he wasn't principally dedicated to the mile, having won Olympic firsts in the 1500, 5000 and 10,000-meter runs in the 1924 and 1928 games, but he was the man who brought excitement to the mile competition.

The first great miler was an Englishman named W. G. George, who covered the 5280 feet in 4:18.4 back in 1885.

Interest in the milers was at fever peak in the 1930s, and the best in America were these three — Glenn Cunningham, Bill Bonthron and Gene Venzke — completing the first lap in that order in a 1934 meet.

Ten years later Thomas Conneff checked in with a 4:15.6. It wasn't until 1913 that the time was lowered again when John P. Jones of Cornell finished in 4:14.4. His racing rival, Norman Tabor of Brown University, cut it again in 1915 with 4:12.6. And there the mark stayed until Nurmi brought the mile to life in 1924.

Nurmi, one of the sports world's heroes during the roaring Twenties, didn't disappoint his many followers. He came through with a new record — 4:10.4, more than two full seconds off the previous mark.

The attention of the sports world turned to the mile. More competitors

From New Zealand came Jack Lovelock, mile record-holder in the early 1930s.

Bill Bonthron, one of Princeton's finest athletes.

geared themselves for the grueling run. And the world-wide concentrated effort began to pay off. A Frenchman, Jules Ladoumegue, became the first man to break 4:10 when he finished in 4:09.2 in 1931.

And then came a brief period of spirited competition in the early 1930s which saw the record mark eclipsed twice in one year — 1933.

Bill Bonthron of Princeton finished with 4:08.7. Later that year a New Zealander, Jack Lovelock, came home in 4:07.6.

Then a confident, determined miler appeared on the scene. Glenn Cunningham, destined to become one of the world's finest racers, brought the mile time down to 4:06.8 in 1936 and fans were beginning to wonder if a four-minute mile were possible.

Cunningham was the last American miler to hold the world's mark. Since Cunningham's championship effort, the mile title has been held by representatives of three countries, England, Sweden and Australia.

The man who wrested supremacy away from America's runners was Sidney Wooderson of England. In 1937 he clipped four-tenths second off Cunningham's mark and the time for the mile was now 4:06.4. The amazing thing about Wooderson's achievement was that he scored his triumph at the comparatively old age of thirty-one. Most of the milers reach their peak in the middle twenties.

Despite the efforts of various top milers from every country in the world the mark stayed at 4:06.4. Then Gunder Haegg came into the picture in 1942. That was the year he brought the record down to 4:04.6 and once again the talk of a four-minute mile was heard.

At the same time another Swede came into the spotlight, a broad-chested youngster named Arne Andersson. And the two Norsemen staged spectacular battles as they aimed for the magic four minutes.

Andersson gained the first advantage when he cut two seconds off his rival's mark, setting the record at 4:02.6, in 1943. The following year the all-round athlete clipped another full second off his own mark and now the record was but one and six-tenths second over the four-minute goal.

Now it was Haegg's turn. In 1945 the ex-lumberjack made it in 4:01.4 and the world waited for him or Andersson to break the barrier. But it wasn't to be.

Both Haegg and Andersson ran afoul

Gunder Haegg was known as the Swedish "wonder" runner. But no matter how hard he tried he never could break the four-minute mile barrier.

Roger Bannister, left, and John Landy both bettered four minutes in this famous duel in 1954. Bannister came from behind to whip the Australian whippet.

of the amateur laws and were barred from racing. When they left, the dreams of the four-minute mile went with them. For seven years there was little excitement on the scene and then suddenly three names appeared. Roger Bannister, an Englishman from Oxford; John Landy, Australian; Wes Santee, an American. Now it became a three-way assault on the four-minute mile.

Little by little they inched up on Haegg's record. Each hit 4:04. Then they got in under 4:03. Each race was excitement because the crowd wanted one of the three fleet flyers to hit the four-minute mark.

Santee did 4:02.4. Landy did 4:02.2.

Then on May 6, 1954 it happened. Roger Bannister attained the unattainable. He breezed home in 3:59.4. The track and field world went wild. Bannister opened up a whole new vista for running accomplishments. As a fitting note, the triumph was made at Oxford, the birthplace of the Amateur Athletic Association in England.

Glenn Cunningham and Gunder Haegg both commented that they had felt that the four-minute mile was a mental goal rather than a physical one.

Cunningham said, "We're still a long way from the best that can be done, now that the psychological barrier has been cleared."

Landy made Cunningham seem like a prophet and he didn't waste much time doing it. That very same year, Landy raced in Finland and cracked Bannister's record. It now stood at 3:58.

Santee tried valiantly to get in under

American mile hopes were wrapped up in Wes Santee, who won many a mile but never beat the magic four-minute figure.

The fastest of them all is Herb Elliott, shown here in a race at Bakersfield, Calif., in which he "loafed" through a 4:01.4 mile.

the four-minute mile but he never could quite bring it off although he twice finished under 4:01.

In 1955, Laszlo Tabori, a 24-year-old Hungarian soldier, broke four minutes by pounding home in 3:59. The four-minute mile was no longer out of man's reach. Who would come along as Nurmi had, and later Cunningham and Haegg and Andersson, to inject new thrills into racing? The answer wasn't long in coming. He was Herb Elliott, the amazing Australian.

From the very beginning Elliott ran the mile as if he owned it. He became the youngest four-minute man at the age of nineteen when he turned in a 3:59.9. Then he chopped it down to 3:58.7, just

five days later.

At the age of twenty he smashed his fellow countryman's record by completing the mile in 3:57.9. But he wasn't through yet. In August of 1958 during the games at Dublin, Elliott, the oat-eating, nut-chewing youngster ripped off a fantastic 3:54.5., a mark that even Ripley wouldn't have believed.

But there it was, 3:54.5. Can the powerful youngster from Down Under reach 3:50? Many authorities think he can. Or will it be some unknown youngster now on a high-school team who will flash through someday in 3:50? It seems definitely within man's reach, It's only a question of time.

Elliott, left, and fellow countryman Merv Lincoln speed toward the finish line, both on their way to superlative performances. Elliott's time was 3:58.7; Lincoln lagged with 3:59.

Some of the Greats

Gordien *McKinley* *Thomas* *Dillard* *Whitfield* *Buddy Davis* *Morrow* *Richards* *Nurmi* *Thorpe* *Bannister* *Cunningham* *Johnson* *Paddock* *Owens* *Elliott* *Delaney* *Courtney* *Mathias* *Haegg* *Warmerdam* *Glenn Davis*

WHAT QUALIFIES A track and field athlete to be considered a "great" performer? Consistency of performance and record-breaking achievement are perhaps the two main factors in judging the greatness of an athlete. However, records are made to be broken, and just about every one has been shattered as one generation replaces another.

The athlete of twenty-five years ago can no longer compare to today's well-trained, supremely-conditioned performer. But who can accurately estimate the "true" abilities of the athlete of the mid-1930s if he were exposed to the training methods and techniques of the 1960s. Are we building faster runners, springier jumpers, superhuman throwers? According to performances, we seem to be producing a superior breed of athletes but it's questionable as to whether some of the record-breakers of today would be turning in the same performances if competing in the 1930s. Therefore, any compilation of great athletes must include those who were superior to all others in their specialities — regardless of the era, the competition, or the prevailing conditions and techniques.

Great miler Bobby Morrow breaks the tape 9.3 to tie the world's record. Story of Morrow page 224.

Down through the years there has been a steady procession of track and field greats who captured the hearts and imaginations of the sport fans of the world. Every nation had its own heroes who went on to win international fame.

The first modern great who stirred the world with his outstanding achievements was an American — **Jim Thorpe.** Thorpe, an exceptional football and baseball player, was the man King Gustav once called "the finest athlete in the world." The Swedish ruler knew what he was talking about.

During the 1912 Olympics Jim astounded coach Mike Murphy by doing most of his training flat on his back in a hammock.

"I've seen some queer birds in my day but your Indian beats all," Mike told famous coach Pop Warner, an Olympic "chaperone."

"With all his football, lacrosse, baseball and track back at school, how could he be out of shape?" Warner wanted to know.

Whenever Jim did come out for practice he'd study the broad jump take-off

Home from the Olympic triumphs of 1912 comes Jim Thorpe, right, talking with Pop Warner, his famous football coach.

and walk off twenty-three. feet. He'd drop a handkerchief there and come back for a jump, always clearing the handkerchief. With Jim, who seldom cared for any training rules, practice was 90 per cent concentration.

Jim was an exuberant spirit with an excess of energy driving in his system. When he trained with the New York Baseball Giants in 1916 he used to pick a teammate and wrestle him to the ground. One by one he'd pick his way through the whole squad. Manager John McGraw had a rule prohibiting any of his players to roughhouse with the flamboyant Indian.

He was a great baseball player but only fair by big-league standards. Grantland Rice selected Thorpe as halfback on his all-time All-America team along with such grid stars as Sammy Baugh, Red Grange and Bronko Nagurski.

He excelled at the native Indian game, lacrosse, while performing at Carlisle. Whatever game he took up he became a superior performer. Billiards, tennis or swimming, it made no difference to the fiery Sac-Fox chieftain.

Many sports fans were stunned and saddened when Thorpe's 1912 Olympic trophies were taken away from him. Many felt it was unfair because the practice of college ball players playing for hotel teams for monetary remuneration was quite prevalent. But the Amateur Athletic Union ordered that Thorpe be barred, and rescinded his trophies.

Behind him Thorpe left romantic memories of a free-wheeling, individualistic athlete who lived by his own rules,

and exciting statistics which can only hint at his superb physical abilities.

Grantland Rice called Thorpe this country's greatest all-round athlete and probably the greatest athlete the world has ever known.

Charley Paddock was the next American who was spotlighted for his achievements. Billed as "The World's Fastest Human," Charley defeated all his competitors whenever a crowd gathered and the pressure was on.

Some thought Cheerful Charley was a grandstander. He employed a sudden,

The finishing kick of the "World's Fastest Human," Charley Paddock.

lunging thrust as he crossed the finish line. Critics said it was a freak finish for a freak performer, but Charley said it gave him an extra burst and enabled him to set record after record.

They set various different distances and Charley, nattily attired in his baby-blue trunks and white shoes, ran them faster than anyone around. He set records for 90 yards (08.8); 110 yards (10.2); 125 yards (12.0); 130 yards (12.4); 150 yards (14.2); 200 yards (19.0); 300 yards (30.2), and 300 meters (33.2). They were all unofficial as track records but they brought the crowd in whenever it was announced that Charley was running.

Charley won the 1920 Olympics 100-meter dash and during the 1924 games he was leading in the 200 contest by a good bit when suddenly he turned around to see if anyone were close. Someone was. It was little Jackson Scholz. As Paddock lost a step by turning, Scholz whizzed by on Charley's "blind side" and roared home to victory.

Although his Olympic record shows only one win, Charley took on all comers throughout his career and until he retired he was track's most colorful performer and top drawing card.

Paavo Nurmi, the Flying Finn, also made his debut in the 1920 Olympics and made his presence felt by winning the 10,000-meter and 10,000-meter cross-country. Nurmi, born in 1897, established 19 records for distances ranging from 1500 to 20,000 meters. His long effortless stride was the model most youthful r a c e r s designed themselves after.

Whenever he trained, which was constantly, Paavo carried with him a large watch which he'd glance at to see exactly how he was pacing himself. He ran to and from work, regularly glancing at his time-piece to check his condition against the elapsed time.

A distance runner primarily, Nurmi came to America for a visit, and raced sixty-nine times in four months. He won all except once when he attempted the comparatively short distance of a half-mile and was edged in a close contest.

The great Paavo Nurmi on his way to victory in the 5000 meters in the 1928 Olympics.

During the height of his fame, Paavo dieted on fruits and nuts and was painfully shy about publicity. Reporters and photographers frightened him and whenever they approached he'd try to duck out and scamper away as fast as his sinewy legs could carry him.

His rigid training program which covered miles of cross-country running over the rugged Finland countryside kept Nurmi sleek and powerful. He was never known to slack off in his untiring efforts to stay at his peak. One time he sat down with friends and ate a rather heavy meal, which, for him, was an unusual occurrence. After rising from the table he realized he had eaten too much.

"I'll have to sweat this vile stuff out of my system," he said. With that he turned and raced the eleven miles back to his home.

An extremely modest person, Nurmi has been quoted as saying he didn't think he ever could have broken the four-minute mile. He also modestly states that Emil Zatopek, the Czechoslovakian long-distance sensation, would be beyond his reach.

True or not, it would be hard to convince anybody who saw the 1924 Olympics when Paavo won three races that anyone could be better than Nurmi.

Today Nurmi is a wealthy builder who lives in a beautiful home in a pine forest beside the sea in Finland.

They called **Glenn Cunningham** "The Kansas Powerhouse" and certainly the sturdy, well-built speedster fit the name better than anyone else.

Crippled as a child when his school-

Fire-scarred legs notwithstanding, Glenn Cunningham was the finest of all competitive milers.

house burned to the ground, Glenn went on to world-wide fame as a miler. Doctors feared he would never walk again, but a determined youth such as Glenn was couldn't be kept down. He learned to walk all over again and then he began to run. He ran to restore his strength and his confidence.

How well he ran is told in the records. He broke 4:10 for the mile twenty times, a notable achievement for that era. In 1934 he held the world's mile record with 4:06.8 that stood for three years.

Glenn had the reputation as a hard-luck guy. Twice in one year he finished second to Bill Bronthon and Jack Lovelock in the metric mile, each time breaking the existing record as he finished in the runner-up spot.

Glenn never smoked nor drank and exemplified the spirit of an American boy who overcame handicaps to go on to world-wide fame as a courageous athlete.

Jesse Owens' finest hour was May 25, 1935, when he broke five world marks and tied a sixth in a Western Conference meet. One of his records came over the 220-yard low hurdles.

The greatness of **Jesse Owens** was established early as he set the national record for high school athletes by doing 220 yards in 20.7 seconds. Owens' achievements under the eyes of Hitler and his future war lords in the 1936 Olympics in Berlin must rate close to the top in any compilation of track and field accomplishments.

While Hitler was shouting his Nordic supremacy creed, Owens, a talented, soft-spoken Negro, was letting his actions speak for themselves. He covered the 100 meters in 9.3, a record he shares with four others. His time for the 220 meters was 20.7. That stood until 1956 when speedster Bobby Morrow sliced a tenth of a second off the mark.

His fantastic broad jump leap of 26 feet, 5¼ inches performed before a hostile crowd and against a talented adversary hasn't even been approached, as far as Olympic competition is concerned. His world record is even better, 26 feet, 8¼ inches.

To give a further idea of Owens' broad-jumping accomplishments, it should be noted that no other Olympic performer had ever topped the 26-foot mark in competition until Ralph Boston turned the trick in the 1960 Olympics at Rome, Italy with a jump of 26 feet, 7¾ inches.

This mark, as well as the others, was set by Owens under trying conditions that might possibly have spurred him on. Hitler refused to acknowledge him and left before he had to congratulate him.

Owens' long stride off the mark usually got him away in front.

The crowd was silent because they feared any display of enthusiasm would be noted by Hitler and his agents.

In addition, Germany's great jumper Lutz Long was at his best. He broke the record that existed at the time. Despite this, or because of it, Owens swept away his opposition and became one of the greatest names in the athletic world.

Today Owens is a successful executive in the Chicago area.

The next track super-star came galloping out of the snow-covered forests of Sweden. He was **Gunder (The Wonder) Haegg.**

Haegg, who worked as a lumberjack with his father, began early. He ran to and from work, a distance of several miles across the frozen countryside. His father set up special courses for him and

Fastest miler in the early 1940s was the slender Swede, Gunder Haegg. He always looked haggard and worn but his thin legs carried him closer to the four-minute barrier than any runner of his time.

timed them as Gunder showed amazing speed and great endurance. Most of the training was done on graded uphills which later made the race courses seem simple by comparison.

Gunder was the first genuine hope for the four-minute mile. He hit 4:04.6 in 1942 and lowered it slowly until he had attained a 4:01.4 mile in 1945.

Between 1941 and 1945 Haegg set world records in seven events from 1500 meters to 5000 meters. He was barred from competing in amateur athletics because of an infraction of the amateur code.

Many observers felt that this disbarment took the life and spirit out of Haegg and prevented him from running a 4:00 mile, even though if he had, it would have to be an unofficial record.

However someone did come along to crack the four-minute mile, **Roger Bannister.** Bannister, an aloof young man, was never considered "one of the boys." But personality in social gathering has little bearing on athletic performances.

As opposed to Haegg and Arne Andersson and nearly all the great milers who worked very long and hard, Bannister had a moderate training schedule. For him it worked wonders. He had only three training sessions a week of one hour each, followed by not more than one race every two weeks.

When Bannister first visited America in 1949 he did the mile in 4:11.9, the fastest it had ever been done by anyone under twenty-one. Five years later he came bursting through with a 3:59.4 and racing had reached a new milestone.

First under the four-minute wire in the mile was England's Roger Bannister.

Improving on Bannister's mark was
John Landy of Australia.

John Landy, who lowered the mark to
3:58 the same year, was a consistently
good performer. The Australian seldom
ran a bad race and threatened to lower
the mark even more. But then out of the
pack came a fellow Australian, **Herb
Elliott,** probably the most amazing athlete ever.

"The only way to beat him is to tie
his legs," said outstanding miler Ron
Delaney.

And that seems to be the only way.
Ten straight times the sturdy furniture
dealer's son ran the mile and ten straight
times he finished in less than four minutes, topping it off with his amazing
3:54.5 in Dublin in August, 1958.

Elliott explained his training schedule
and made it known that he is from the
school that feels that hard work is the
only answer. His diet may not be found
on the menus in the better hotel restau-
rants but it's worked wonders for him.

"I eat raw oats with raisins, nuts and
bananas mixed in," he said. "That's for
breakfast and a lot of Australian runners
like it. Hard work is the only way to do
anything. You have to be hard on your-
self."

Some authorities have said that Elliott
drives himself beyond human endurance. It's been reported that he gallops
fourteen miles along the sandy Australian shores right after breakfast and col-
lapses to the ground to re-gather his energy. Then he gets up and roars up steep
sand dunes. Once he raced up and down
a steep sand dune forty-two times in succession. When exhausted he climbs into

222

Most perfect mile running machine of the first sixty years of the 20th century has been Herb Elliott.

a sleeping bag and dozes for an hour. He awakens, has a lunch of raw carrots, cabbage, brown bread, cheese and milk and is off and running again. He tapers off his day's workouts with some heavy weight-lifting.

When not racing Elliott works as a clerk in a chemical company in Australia and looks not at all like the toughest, fastest miler the world has yet produced.

"You get sick of training," Herb has stated, "but that's the time when you stick to it. That's when one runner proves himself better than the others. Anyone can do it when he's enthusiastic. It's when you stick to it that you show you're the s u p e r i o r man. Sometimes you're just dying to stop training, but you keep going. It's a matter of will power."

Elliott, who has the will power to keep training and get the most out of his ability, has never been beaten at his specialty, the mile.

Well-built at 5 feet, 11 inches and 150 pounds, Herb is the chief threat to the 3:50 mile "the ultimate in human performance." Of course, that was said about the four-minute mile.

As for Herb, his comment is:

"Who can be sure what the ultimate is?"

He plans to keep on trying, along with the thousands of other milers from all over the world, to continue the march showing man's improvement in physical capabilities, reaching and then topping "the ultimate in human performance."

Ron Delany, who came across the sea from his native Ireland to set track records for Villanova University, never worries about his finishing time. All he thinks of is winning. And he does that with great regularity.

But while he wins, he also sets more than his share of records. He holds the Olympic record for the 1500-meter run and owns the world indoor mile record with 4:02.5.

He won three straight IC4A mile crowns and four successive NAAU indoor championships and each time he set a new record. In addition, he built a record of thirty-six consecutive races without a defeat. While racing under the Villanova banner, Ron won ten first place medals tying the record for the most IC4A victories.

Ron is a post-graduate student at Villanova, studying Dramatic Arts.

Handsome **Bobby Morrow,** called by many "the greatest sprinter of all time," is the first athlete to win three gold medals in Olympic Games competition since Jesse Owens turned the trick in 1936.

During the 1956 games at Melbourne, Bobby tied the 100-meter mark of 10.3, set a new 200-meter record with 20.6 and was anchor man in the relay team which set still another mark, 39.5 seconds for the 400-meter distance.

At high school in his native Harlingen, Texas, Bobby was a star tailback and captain of his football team as well as the mainstay of his track team.

Bobby, who attended Abilene Christian College, is a member of the Church of Christ and teaches a Bible class each Sunday.

Bobby lives in Texas with his bride, his former high school classmate, and their two children.

Ron Delaney holds two records — the Olympic 1500 meter and the indoor mile event.

The discus is on its way as Rafer Johnson shatters the decathlon record.

Not only is **Rafer Johnson** one of the greatest all-around young athletes in American history, he is an outstanding student.

While Rafer was earning eleven letters in football, baseball, track and basketball in Kingsburg. (California) High School, he also served as president of the student body in his senior year.

Rafer continued his exceptional work in both athletics and education when he went to U.C.L.A. He shattered Bob Mathias' decathlon mark when he scored 7983 points competing in the Central California AAU meet. He raised his record point total in the USA-Russia track meet held in Moscow in 1958, with a mark of 8302 points.

Some of Rafer's best performances include a 25-foot, 5¾-inch broad jump; 243-foot, 10½-inch javelin throw and a 22.7 second mark in the 220-yard low hurdles.

In his senior year at U.C.L.A., Rafer repeated the honor he won in high school, being elected president of the student body.

Rafer, a native of Hillsboro, Texas, stands six feet, three inches and weighs 200 pounds.

Tom Courtney, winner of the 800-meter race during the 1956 Olympics at Melbourne, has run the fastest half-mile ever performed on a flat track — a 1:52.6 mark.

Tom offers this formula for his success: "I don't like to run behind anyone and I hate to be passed." To put this into action Tom makes sure he gets a fast jump at the start and runs at a steady pace to keep the lead, which he does most of the time.

His reluctance to trail at the start stems from a racing incident during his school days at Caldwell High in New Jersey. Tom was knocked to the ground in a scramble and was out of the race. He vowed he'd never let that happen again.

Tom, the only Fordham University athlete ever to win an Olympic Gold Medal, was anchor man in his school's record-setting relay team. The quartet ran the two miles in 7:27.3.

Al Oerter is another one of the great track and field athletes who did their performing under the banner of Kansas University.

A student at the school which produced such stars as Glenn Cunningham and Wes Santee, Al became the second Kansas star to win an Olympic Gold Medal by taking the discus prize in 1956 at Melbourne when he was a sophomore. At that time he defeated world's record-holder Fortune Gordien with a heave of 184 feet, 10½ inches.

Oerter, a firm believer in weight-lifting to build strength for competitive sports, still holds the national freshman record (171 feet, 6 inches) and the national prep school record (184 feet, 2¾ inches.) His best collegiate toss was 188 feet, 2 inches, a mark he reached twice as a senior.

Bob Mathias was one of the greatest of decathlon performers. He was also an excellent hurdler.

Some people say **Bob Mathias** is the greatest all-round athlete who ever lived. Certainly he must be considered as one of the best.

A handsome, well-built youngster at seventeen, Bob came out of Tulare (California) High School in 1948 and went to London where he won the Olympic decathlon. In 1952 he became the first man ever to win two straight Olympic decathlons.

At Stanford University Bob led his school to outstanding victories. In one meet he scored 28 of his team's 74 points in a fantastic performance which saw him take first places in the shot, discus, pole vault, high and low hurdles, and finish second in the high jump.

In addition, Bob starred for Stanford's football team during his junior year.

After college, Bob launched a new career as a television personality and had his own sports show in California.

Another Olympic record holder is Al Oerter, who made his mark in the discus.

226

When **John Thomas** high-jumped seven feet in early 1959 he shattered another theory devised by experts who said man could never jump that high.

Just to prove it was no fluke, John added an inch and a quarter to that mark the very next month.

John began setting records at Rindge Technical High School in Boston. His finest mark as a scholastic performer was 6 feet, 7⅝ inches in the N.A.A.U. Schoolboy Meet. Since he began at Boston University he has been unbeatable in his specialty. In addition, he also won six hurdle races during his freshman season.

Boston University Athletic Director Vic Stout said that in addition to Thomas' ability to work and train with determination, his technique of relaxing while under competitive pressure is a big factor in his success.

John, who plans on becoming a teacher-coach after he is graduated in 1962, is looking onward and upward. He says the eight-foot jump is not beyond man's reach.

No American has ever jumped higher than John Thomas.

After **Harrison Dillard** was graduated from high school he hoped to get into a major college to continue his track career, but the coaches told him he was too small.

He was only 5 feet, 10 inches and most of the great hurdlers were over six feet, a height which enabled them to clear the high barriers and take only three big steps between each hurdle.

Harrison wrote to Track Coach Eddie Finnigan at little Baldwin-Wallace. Immediately after looking at Dillard, Coach Finnigan predicted he had a new champion on his hands.

They worked long and hard and in 1947 Harrison fulfilled his coach's predictions, running the 220-yard low hurdles in 22.3. In 1948 he shattered the high hurdle mark by breezing home in 13.6.

In the 1948 Olympics, Harrison won the 100-meter sprint and was on the championship 400-meter relay team, thereby winning gold medals in two of the events won by his boyhood idol, Jesse Owens, in the Olympics twelve years earlier.

Harrison Dillard overcame a height handicap and became a champion.

Glenn Davis, a Sullivan Trophy winner for his excellence in track, is a racer who exudes determination and power.

A fine student of running, Glenn is the greatest quarter-miler in the world, setting a mark of 45.7. Some experts look for him to get even better.

Glenn has amazing recuperative powers and requires only a brief rest after an exhausting race in order to re-gather his strength for another event. He is a graduate of Ohio State University.

Glenn Davis exhibits his flawless hurdling technique.

228

Mal Whitfield was an almost perfect example of a human running machine. To him, racing was a science to be studied. When he prepared for a race he concentrated so much on getting ready he would often fail to recognize friends when passing them on the street.

His easy, effortless style was a model for other runners who watched Mal glide home first in the middle-distance events from 300 to 1000 yards. During his training season, Mal ran a minimum of six miles daily. He was graduated from Ohio State University in 1947.

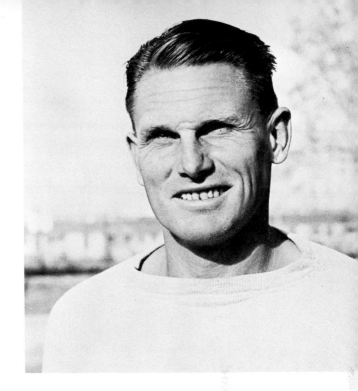

Cornelius Warmerdam, first to pole vault higher than fifteen feet.

Mal Whitfield, the master planner.

Cornelius Warmerdam was the first athlete to shatter a man-made "ceiling" for any athletic event.

Before Warmerdam padded down the runway, experts said man was capable of clearing only 14 feet, 11 inches in the pole vault. But on April 13, 1940, Cornelius cleared fifteen feet and continued on from there.

By the time he was through, the Flying Dutchman from Fresno State College had lifted the pole vault mark to a world record high.

After he retired, Cornelius, a former basketball star in college, coached his alma mater in both basketball and track and field. One of his students was the 1953 NCAA champ Fred Barnes.

In 1957 Bob Gutowski broke the Dutchman's fabulous record. Cornelius commented: "Good, it's about time."

229

Polio couldn't defeat Buddy Davis.

Walter (Buddy) Davis' career tells a story filled with courage and hope.

At the age of eight he was stricken with paralysis and lost the power of his legs. For a time it looked as if he would never walk again. Then gradually he began to regain control of his limbs. When he returned to school, he could walk only short distances. When he tired, the older boys would carry him about.

As he grew he developed strength in his legs. He was always tall and lanky and as a result never thought he'd amount to much in track or field. One day he tried

high jumping and found he was a natural. In a short time he led his Texas high school team to a championship.

He received a basketball scholarship to Texas A & M and went out for track only to strengthen his legs for the cage sport. He developed rapidly. As a sophomore, he jumped 6 feet, 4 inches. Each year he continued to better this mark. Buddy set an AAU mark of 6 feet, 10½ inches and won the 1956 Olympic event with an effort of 6 feet, 8.32 inches.

Fortune Gordien, the world's discus throwing champion, was an all-round athlete in his youth. He was swimming champion at the age of thirteen, played football with the city champions of Minneapolis, Minnesota, was an excellent tumbler, wrestler and at the age of fourteen won the city's drop-kicking and punting competition.

At the University of Minnesota Fortune played freshman football, then gave it up to concentrate on track and field.

He set the world's record for the discus in 1949 with a heave of 185 feet. Later, he increased this to 186 feet, 11 inches. In 1953 he added more distance with a toss of 194 feet, 6 inches, a record going into the 1960's. So Gordien set three world's marks in this event.

Fortune still spends much of his free time working with track and field athletes from high schools and colleges, helping them to develop championship technique.

He lives in Altadena, California, with his wife and four children and is associated with an organization of artistic designers and consultants.

Herb McKenley had a giant stride.

Herb McKenley is another product of the University of Illinois, a school that has produced many great athletes.

A native of Jamaica, Herb left his homeland to star for Illinois' track team in 1946 and 1947. During his career he won the 440-yard crown in Big Ten competition for both indoor and outdoor racing. As a junior, he broke the outdoor 440 mark with a sparkling 46.2. The following year he set the indoor mark of 48.1 seconds.

During the 1948 Olympics, Herb raced under the Jamaica banner and was on the winning 400-meter relay team.

Herb is now an athletic supervisor in Jamaica.

The Rev. **Bob Richards,** known as the "pole-vaulting Parson," has cleared fifteen feet more than any other man in history.

Two-time pole vault king was Bob Richards.

While attending high school in his native Champaign, Illinois, Richards starred as quarterback on the football team as well as heading the track squad. After high school he attended the University of Illinois where he began setting records with his lofty leaps.

During his collegiate career, Richards won the American decathlon championship three times, attesting to his all-round athletic ability. After graduating from college in 1947, he entered the 1948 Olympics and finished third in the decathlon. In 1952 and 1956 he easily won the pole-vaulting competition.

An ordained minister of the Church of the Brethren, the reverend has his own church near Los Angeles. He also is a leader in the national program for physical fitness among American youth.

Olympics

Most significant of all international sports competition are the Olympic Games, a series of sports events for amateur athletes of all nations. They are held every four years and are run by a completely international governing body.

The Olympic Games have their own symbol, a series of five linked rings which represent the five major continents of the world. The rings are linked together to denote the sporting friendship of the people of the earth. Beneath these five rings appears the Olympic motto—*Citius, Altius, Fortius*—"swifter," "higher," "stronger." Thus, run faster, jump higher and throw more strongly.

The founder of the modern Olympic Games was Baron Pierre de Coubertin, a French nobleman and sportsman. He also wrote the Olympic Creed, which reads, "The important thing in the Olympic Games is not winning but taking part. The essential thing in life is not conquering but fighting well." Unfortunately this excellent bit of philosophy has since been ignored and disregarded by so many.

The story of the Olympics is one of the most romantic in all of sport. It is full of hopes and disappointments, successes and failures. And it is also the faraway dream of every young track and field athlete to one day become a part of this greatest of sports dramas.

234

America in the Olympics

MORE THAN ANY OTHER event, the Olympic Games bring attention and fame to athletic standouts. The international competitions held every four years is the World Series of track and field.

Since the first modern Olympics held in Athens, Greece, in 1896, the United States has always been the most consistent of winners.

There was no organized effort to field a team for the Athens contest. Groups volunteered strictly on their own and began raising money for the trip across. The Boston Athletic Association thought that a few of its athletes might do well and they made arrangements to enter the competition. A Princeton track star named Robert S. Garrett thought he'd like to try his hand and he joined up. A Harvard student named James B. Connolly applied for a leave of absence from school and when he was refused, he simply walked out of school and started in the general direction of Athens.

Connolly went on to become the first U.S. winner. The hop-step-jump was the first contest of the day and he outdistanced all competitors with a mark of 45 feet. He was the first of nine olive wreath winners for the U.S. during the first games.

Garrett won the shot put and the discus throw. The U.S. lost only three events, the 800 meters, 1500 meters and the marathon run, taken by S. Loues of Greece.

Loues was a slim little shepherd who came down from the hills determined to win for the honor of Greece which had thus far been shut out. No one gave him much of a chance. For two nights before the race he prayed for strength to win. The day before he fasted completely, not eating anything for twenty-four hours before the race.

Under a boiling sun, Loues came from behind to whip some highly-touted competitors to make good his vow and Greece had a winner.

The Paris games in 1900 were handled with an air of mystery that almost amounted to complete secrecy. The American winners who were given their medals learned only then that they were competing in the Olympics. They thought they were taking part in an athletic festival that was part of the Paris Exposition.

Newspapers and programs made no mention that these were the Olympics. The fifty-five American athletes who crossed the Atlantic for the games were never told that they would be battling for Olympic championships. But it apparently mattered very little, for the U.S. took seventeen events, losing only five.

While the Americans were still unorganized, the foreign competitors had even less of a cohesive unit. Many of them were ill-equipped and some countries only sent one or two athletes.

Dorando Pietri seems to be first over the finish line in the marathon of 1908. But he didn't win because officials helped him across.

Alvin Kraenzlein of Penn, described earlier as the "father of the hurdles," set a record by winning four championships, the 60-meter dash, the 110 and 200-meter hurdles and the running broad jump.

It was at these Olympics that the U.S. unveiled Ray Ewry, a tall, slim athlete who was an invalid as a small boy. Urged by his doctors to do leg-strengthening exercises, Ewry went on to win ten Olympic championships, more than any other athlete. In 1900 he won the standing broad jump, the standing high jump and the standing hop-step-jump.

A burly New York A. C. man, John J. Flanagan, was the only non-college man to win a point by tossing the hammer 167 feet, 4 inches. The only foreign hammer throwers, both Swedes, were so wild that every time they threw it sent the audience into a near panic. They recorded no hits, but they did have a couple of near misses.

In 1904 the Olympic Games came to America for the first time. They were held in St. Louis and the U.S. virtually ran away with all honors, taking 21 out of 22 events.

As in the other earlier games there was very little semblance of order. Neither France nor Great Britain sent any athletes over to compete and many U.S. colleges, which had participated earlier, refused to send representatives. But from the U.S. standpoint, things were taking shape. For the first time the American squad was composed of athletes sent by athletic clubs from all over the country. It was the first truly All-American squad.

The U.S. boasted four triple winners, Archie Hahn, H. L. Hillman, James Lightbody and Ray Ewry, who made it a total of six Olympic crowns.

But despite the performances of these athletes the spotlight focused on the marathon. Certainly it boasted the most colorful personality. He was Felix Carvajal, a Cuban mailman who told his fellow citizens in Havana that he wanted to run in the Olympics. To raise money for his efforts he ran around and around a public square until people came and tossed money to him. When he had

John Flanagan won hammer throw in 1900 Olympics.

raised enough, he took a boat to New Orleans.

There unfortunately, he fell afoul of a few shady characters, who lured the under-sized postman into a game of chance. In a short time Felix was again without funds. And it was still a long way to St. Louis. So he headed north, running, walking, hitch-hiking. He reached St. Louis, hungry and tired. He applied for admission to the race and they let him enter.

He never had any handling and didn't even own a pair of running shorts. One of the other athletes took a pair of scissors and snipped Felix's trousers and they became his racing togs. He was penniless, but his laughing personality won him many friends and they saw to it that he was well-provided for.

The race began and Felix jogged along the road, cracking jokes in Spanish with the spectators lined along the way. If he spotted an apple tree he'd stop, climb up, grab a few and run off, munching the fruit as he ran.

It would be a fitting climax to the story if Felix won, but he didn't. He did, however, finish fourth, a remarkable accomplishment for the untrained, laughing Cuban who had become a favorite with the crowd.

A South African named Lentauw operated a concession in Paris during the 1900 games and was intrigued by the marathon. He journeyed to St. Louis and entered. He finished twelfth and might have done better were it not for the fact that a growling German Shepherd took an instant dislike to him and chased him a mile off the course, over fences, through meadows and down back alleys.

The heat of the day was intense, but the dust raised by chugging autos that accompanied the runners was even worse. Only 14 of the 31 starters finished. Despite the wild activities that had gone before the climax was still to come.

Fred Lorz of the Mohawk A. C. had run about nine miles when he doubled over with severe stomach cramps. Lorz decided not to go on. He hailed one of the dust-raising, chugging cars and hitched a ride. He waved to the runners as he passed them along the route, shouting encouragement to them, urging them on to greater effort. As he was driven to within five miles of the finish line the auto gave up. Lorz stepped out, still in his racing outfit, and began running to keep from catching cold and stiffening up. He trotted the five miles back to the stadium far ahead of any of the others. When the crowd saw him they began cheering.

The officials gathered around him and prepared to announce him as the winner. Just as the award was about to be presented someone called Lorz a fake. Just then the real winner, T. J. Hicks, staggered into the stadium.

Angrily turning away from Lorz, the officials prepared to award the prize to Hicks. However, just as he was about to be honored, Hicks collapsed and four men had to pick him up and haul him away.

Lorz, who undoubtedly was playing a monumental joke because the other racers and some of the officials along the way knew he was out of the race, was chastised and banned for life by the A.A.U.

So despite the fact that there was a dearth of foreign competitors, the 1904 Olympics will be remembered as the wildest ever.

The Greeks were so eager to hold another Olympics that they didn't wait four years. They held another one in 1906. The U.S. won 11 out of 19 games, featured by Ray Ewry's double triumph, giving him eight Olympic wins. Despite their enthusiasm, the Greeks failed to win an award.

Most notable aspect about the 1906 games from an American point of view was that it marked the first time this country had an Olympic team selected by an American Olympic Committee. It was headed by President Theodore Roosevelt, who served as honorary chairman.

The 1908 games in London were marked by constant bickering and grumbling. Sweden and the United States protested because their flags weren't displayed in the new stadium. Americans protested the entry of Indian Tom Longboat racing for Canada because he had been declared a professional in the U.S. Ireland grumbled because England said Irish athletes would run under the British flag and their points would go toward Great Britain's score. Italians were angered because they charged British officials with interference at the marathon finish line which, they said, deprived their man of victory. Canada and France complained about British rulings in the cycling competition. The Swedes withdrew their wrestlers charging the British judges with unfairness.

The ancient Greeks of long ago considered that the gathering of the world's athletes in competition would increase international good will. If they had been around in 1908 they would have been shocked at what went on. Contrary to promoting understanding, these games contributed to great hostility among the nations.

Finally peace broke out and when the smoke cleared away the U.S. had won 14 out of 24 events, with Great Britain garnering six firsts. Ewry won two more titles, concluding his great career with ten victories.

In the 1912 games at Stockholm the United States, for the first time, failed to win at least half of the contests, taking only 13 out of 28. It was during these Olympics that the first of the Flying Finns flashed into prominence. He was Hannes Kolehmainen who came home first in the 5000, 10,000 meters and the cross-country.

It was during the 1912 games that Jim Thorpe, "The Carlisle Indian," put on an astounding show by winning the decathlon and pentathlon in handy style. When Sweden's King Gustaf V awarded Thorpe first prize he called him "the greatest athlete in the world."

Later Thorpe's prizes were taken back when it was learned that he had received $15 or $30 a week playing professional baseball while at school. There was no attempt to cover up. Thorpe nev-

Jim Thorpe was the main figure in the 1912 Olympics.

er thought he was doing anything wrong. He played the games under his own name and they even appeared in box scores. But everything that was presented to him was taken back.

Jim, in later years, recalling the Olympics and his receiving the award on the winner's platform, said:

"At least they couldn't strip me of the King's words."

The rancor of the London games four years previous had been forgotten and once more all was right with the competing nations, numbering twenty-six.

And for the first time the games directly were responsible for exchanges of visits among various athletes from different countries and friendly trading in techniques. Al Kraenzlein went to Germany in 1913 to help them develop a team, and Finland sent Lauri Pikhala to America to study under famous Olympic coach Mike Murphy.

But in 1914 the war broke out and there was no time for games in 1916. Four years later the Olympics were resumed once again in Antwerp, Belgium.

The Olympics which followed the Armistice introduced one of the all-time greats in racing — Charley Paddock, "the world's fastest human," and Paavo Nurmi, the fleet Finn. Neither disappointed. Paddock won the 100 meters, while Nurmi took the 10,000 meters and the 10,-000-meter cross-country.

The United States planned to make a triumphant return to complete supremacy and fielded a team of 300 athletes. But then trouble broke out. The only vessel available to carry the team across the waters was an army transport. Eating and sleeping arrangements were crude and not conducive to bringing peace of mind to the athletes. And things got worse in war-torn Belgium. The only accommodations were in an empty schoolhouse. This put the already-soured team members into a worse frame of mind. So it was a thoroughly irritated bunch of Americans that took the field when the Olympics began.

And to add to their discomfort, they found that the other nations had come a long way in their training programs. The Scandinavians especially had progressed in their running, and Great Britain field-

Swiftest of the Scandinavians in the 1920 Olympics was Paavo Nurmi, the Flying Finn.

ed several stars. As a result the U.S. made its worst showing in the history of the games, taking eight first places, while losing nineteen. Finland tied this mark of eight, giving that nation its best record in Olympic action.

The most colorful character was an easy-going Italian named Ugo Frigerio.

Loren Murchison, a top sprinter in the 1920's and a member of a U.S. winning Olympic relay team, takes baton from Charlie Paddock.

Ugo was a contestant in the walking events and he insisted on a band playing accompanying music as he strolled around the arena. If the band missed a beat or slackened its tempo Ugo would shake his fist at them and bawl loudly that the band was not of the highest quality. If the crowd didn't cheer him on each trip past the grandstand he'd wake them up with loud yells acclaiming himself. With all his flashiness, Ugo outwalked all his competitors and took first honors in both the 3000 and 10,000-meter walks.

The 1924 games in Paris had but one star — Paavo Nurmi. The untiring, steady-striding Finn who glanced at the stop-watch on his wrist to pace himself as he ran along, won three races, 1500, 5000 and 10,000 meters. And, he set Olympic records in all three races.

With 320 athletes on its roster, the U. S. hoped to get back to its earlier Olympic marks of complete superiority. They fared better, winning thirteen, while the other nations collectively won an equal number. Finland, led by its speedy distance runners headed by Nurmi, equalled its own previous high by winning eight contests.

In 1928 at Amsterdam the stars of early Olympics, Paddock and Nurmi, were both defeated by younger, more powerful rivals. Paddock's specialty, the 100 meters, was won by a 19-year-old Canadian, Percy Williams, while Nurmi lost the 5000 meters to Ville Ritola, another Finn. Paavo, however, still had the stride and the endurance to take the 10,000 meters crown.

The final tallies showed the United States with eight wins out of twenty-two events. Once again, little Finland with a population of only 3,500,000, placed second, garnering five wins.

Record crowds, record receipts and record performances marked the 1932 Olympics at Los Angeles. The location was ideal for the games, featuring a stadium holding 105,000, an auditorium seating 10,000, a swimming stadium with a capacity of 12,000 and an Olympic rowing course on Alamitos Bay with sideline seats for 17,000 spectators.

New records were set in twelve events with Eddie Tolan, a chunky speedster, setting two. He ran the 100 meters in 10.3 and the 200 in 21.2. The closing event, the marathon, was the most exciting in the history of the games. The first four finishers entered the packed stadium all within one minute and five seconds of one another. Winner was Juan Carlos Zabala, a 20-year-old newspaper boy from Argentina. His time of 2 hours, 31 minutes, 36 seconds was another Olympic record.

The 1936 Olympics at Berlin were the most politically significant games. They were held against a background of rising international tensions as Adolph Hitler had come into power in Germany.

Many French people protested the raising of money to send athletes to Germany. The Spanish team, already settled down in the Olympic village awaiting the start of competition, was withdrawn at the last minute because civil war broke out in Spain. Brazil sent two rival teams to Berlin and both were eventually taken out of the competition.

During the formal o p e n i n g ceremonies, v i s i t i n g teams representing countries friendly to Germany gave the Nazi salute and were greeted joyously by the German fans. The nations who were unfriendly with the Germans were received in silence or, as in the case of the United States, greeted by derisive whistles.

At the time also, Hitler had created the theory that the German was a superman and that non-Aryan and non-Nordic peoples were inferior. The results of the games served to blast that theory to pieces very shortly.

The man most responsible for the United States' winning 12 of 23 events was a soft-spoken young man named Jesse Owens, one of America's greatest athletes of all time. Owens set two Olympic records and tied another. His 10.3 tied Tolan's mark for the 100 meters set in 1932. In the 200 meters Owens finished in 20.7, chopping a half-second off Tolan's record. But it was in the running broad jump that Owens achieved unforgettable greatness.

Competing against German ace Lutz Long, who also broke the previous mark, Owens leaped 26 feet, 5 and 5/16 inches, an Olympic mark that still stands.

Hitler ignored Owens by refusing to shake hands with him, but most of the Germans regarded him as a super athlete and Owens became a hero on the streets of Berlin before he returned to America.

When the 1936 games ended there was a lapse of twelve years in the games because of World War Two. Germany, Italy, and Japan continued their aggressiveness against the small nations and soon the whole world was fighting for freedom. After the war ended, London was chosen as the site of the next games, in 1948.

Austerity reigned in war-battered Eng-

Greatest moment for any Olympian is to stand on the victory pedestal. Jesse Owens had this thrill in 1936 after he set a new broad jump record.

land and there was little money to be spent on Olympic festivities. There were few frills or fancy extras during the games but they proved a source of great relaxation and enjoyment to people who were weary of warfare.

The games introduced two more great athletes to the world, Bob Mathias of California and Emil Zatopek of Czecho-slovakia.

The barrel-chested Zatopek intro-duced probably the most ungraceful style of running the world has ever seen but it in no way interfered with his win-ning.

"He runs like a man who'd just been stabbed in the heart," commented one observer after watching the balding

Bob Mathias was only seventeen when he took the decathlon competition in 1948.

Czech bounce and jerk across the finish line to win the 10,000 meters in 29 minutes, 59½ seconds, a new Olympic record. It was at these games that Zatopek established himself as a coming running great.

Mathias, a 17-year-old, proved himself to be the most versatile American athlete since Jim Thorpe. Mathias was a star football and basketball player in California and his ruggedness helped him during his gruelling trials. The decathlon began under rain-filled clouds as 75,000 people jammed into the stadium at 10:30 A.M. The rain began and continued through the morning, afternoon and night.

Throughout the day Mathias sat under a blanket in the rain, coming out only to compete against the world's best. He went through the 100 meters in 11.2 seconds. He ran the 400 in 51.7. In the high jump he cleared 6 feet, 1¼ inches. He put the shot 42 feet, 9¼ inches and then had his first nourishment, a box lunch, while huddling under the blanket.

Mathias' broad jump measured 21 feet, 8½ inches. He did the 110-meter hurdles in 15.7 seconds and threw the discus 144 feet, 4 inches. It was dusk and the rain was still falling heavily when he had to pole vault.

Although the crossbar was a shadowy blur at the end of the runway, Mathias slipped and skidded down the runway and cleared 11 feet, 5¾ inches, higher than anyone else competing.

When the time came for javelin competition it was so dark that the youthful Hercules missed the take-off line entirely. Officials used a flashlight to penetrate the murky gloom so Mathias could stay within the legal bounds for his throws.

The officials announced that Mathias' point total was far ahead of any of his competitors who had wilted long ago, but there was still the 1500-meter run remaining. In the darkness the precocious athlete trotted the distance in 5 minutes, 11 seconds, giving him a winning total of 7139 points.

The 1952 Olympics in Helsinki were opened when Paavo Nurmi, the great runner of the 1920s, ran into the packed stadium with the lighted torch signifying the beginning of the games. To a man, the audience rose and cheered, applauded and wept happily as they honored the man who symbolized the spirit of the Olympics.

As in the 1936 games, the 1952 contests were conducted against an intrigue-filled background. There was conflict on both sides of the Iron Curtain and unrest in various countries throughout the world as communism and democracy battled for economic and political superiority. Victories in the games would be substantial propaganda achievements.

Once again it was Zatopek who was the individual star, but the United States offered numerous standouts, including the Rev. Robert Richards, Parry O'Brien, Mathias and Cy Young, the first American to win the javelin throw.

Zatopek, his face straining and his arms flailing wildly, sailed home first in the 5000, 10,000 meters and the marathon. His marathon mark of 2 hours, 23 minutes, 3.2 seconds still stands.

Rev. Richards won the pole vault with a new high of 14 feet, 11¼ inches, while Parry O'Brien put the shot 57 feet, 1½ inches, another record which he proceeded to break in the 1956 games. Young, the javelin thrower, heaved the spear 242 feet, ¾ inch, again, another Olympic high up to that time.

Horace Ashenfelter, a Federal Bureau of Investigation operator, competed in the 3000-meter steeplechase against the unofficial champion, Vladimir Kasantsev of Russia. It was expected that the newspapers would headline the results by saying, "F.B.I. Man Trails Communist,"

Three-event winner in 1952 was Emil Zatopek of Czechoslovakia, the long-distance runner who defied all proper technique and style.

245

The 1952 Olympics were almost an all-Zatopek show when Dana, the wife of Emil, hurled the javelin to a new women's mark of 165 feet, 7½ inches.

but it wasn't to be. Ashenfelter, true to his profession, was a diligent student of technique. He picked up some clues from friendly Finnish runners and with them he solved the mystery of beating the strong Russian. Not only that, Ashenfelter turned in a record time — 8 minutes, 45.4 seconds.

Another sidelight was the entry of Zatopek's wife, Dana, who threw the javelin 165 feet, 7.05 inches, another rec-

ord. Sports writers couldn't resist calling the Zatopeks, "Czech and double Czech."

When the scorers finished, United States had captured fourteen crowns while the rest of the world divided ten among them.

Mathias made history by becoming the only man ever to win two successive decathlons, capturing the event with a total of 7887 points.

The 1956 games at Melbourne was a peaceful affair that saw its share of records shattered. The United States showed exceptional speed and power in taking 15 of 23 events.

They discovered a new decathlon champion, Milton Campbell, who garnered 7937 points. Rev. Richards and Parry O'Brien both repeated their 1952 wins with outstanding performances. Bobby Morrow set a new standard in the 200 meters, doing it in 20.6 to beat Jesse Owens' mark which had stood for twenty years. Charles Dumas leaped 6 feet, 11¼ inches for a new high jump mark. Sullivan Award Winner Glenn Davis covered the 400-meter hurdles in 50.1 seconds, still another record.

Without a doubt, the Olympic Games have achieved what the ancient Greeks intended them to achieve—new standards in physical attainment and promotion of goodwill among the world's powers through friendly athletic rivalry.

The Olympics must be classified as one of the sports world's outstanding contributions toward the development of civilization.

Glenn Davis clears his last hurdle on the way to breaking the 400-meter record in the 1956 Olympics.

The 1960 Olympics at Rome were marked by tragedy, upsets, a raft of new records and a strong finishing performance by the American track and field forces after a faltering start.

The first death in the history of the Olympics occurred in the cycling event when Knud Enemark Jensen of Denmark collapsed, as did two other members of his team. The event was conducted in intense heat and Jensen, who died in a hospital, was said to have suffered heatstroke. However the coach of the Danish team, after first denying it, admitted that stimulant drugs had been administered to the Danish cyclists.

Upsets occurred in the sprints and high jump. Ray Norton, termed the "world's fastest human" and considered a certain winner in the 100 and 200 meters, could do no better than sixth in both specialties. John Thomas, the 19-year-old Bostonian who had high-jumped better than seven feet more times than anyone in the world, was unanimously picked to take this event, and also set a record in so doing. Thomas, although he did better the Olympic record, had to be content with third place and a bronze medal with a seven-foot, one-quarter inch jump.

American track and field athletes did set eight Olympic records, thus softening somewhat the disappointments of Norton and Thomas, and the failure of Hal Connolly, a prime favorite to capture the hammer throw.

The most significant mark to fall was also the oldest. Ralph Boston of Tennessee State broad-jumped 26 feet, 7¾ inches to erase the record set by Jesse Owens in 1936. Thus none of Owens' Olympic marks are now standing.

Otis Davis won the 400 meters in 44.9 seconds, which was also a world record, and the American relay team of Jack

Yerman, Earl Young, Glenn Davis and
Otis Davis set a record of 3 minutes 2.2
seconds in capturing the 1600 meters.

Lee Calhoun took the 110-meter hurdles but failed to set a record, Glenn
Davis, however, bettered the 400-meter
hurdle mark with a 49.3 performance.
The marvelous Davis thus lowered his
1956 Olympic standard of 50.1 seconds.

Don Bragg, Bill Nieder, Al Oerter and
Rafer Johnson — all gold medalists —
turned in record-breaking performances.
Bragg pole-vaulted 15 feet, $5\frac{1}{8}$ inches;
Bill Nieder put the shot 64 feet, $6\frac{3}{4}$
inches; Al Oerter threw the discus 194
feet, 2 inches and Johnson accumulated
8,392 points in the decathlon.

The women's team was dominated by
Wilma Rudolph, the sleek sprintress
from Tennessee State who took three
gold medals in winning the 100 and 200
meters and serving as anchor on the 400-
meter relay team.

Perhaps the outstanding individual
achievement of the 1960 Olympics was
the 1500-meter performance of Herb Elliott. The Australian running machine
established Olympic and world records
in turning in a 3 minute, 35.6-second
clocking.

Down goes Bragg, above right, and so
does Olympic record. Marine private
Don Bragg of Pennsville, N.J., starts on
his way down after orbiting 14 feet, $5\frac{1}{4}$
inches in the polt vault.

The United States was 1-2-3 in the
discus throw. Leading the parade with
a record toss of 194 feet, 2 inches was
Al Oerter, right, of Long Island, N.Y.

No longer does the name of Jesse Owens dot the Olympic record book. Ralph Boston of Laurel, Miss., left, took care of that when he broad-jumped 26 feet, 7¾ inches to erase the standard set by Owens in the 1936 games.

Boston has since bettered this record with a jump of 27 feet, 1¼ inches in the 1961 A.A.U. meet.

Rafer Johnson, below, earned the right to be known as the world's greatest athlete when he took the 10-event decathlon with a record point total. The Kingsburg (Calif.) iron man had strong opposition from his training mate in the United States, Chuan Kwang Yang, who represented Taiwan (Nationalist China).

A pair of gold medalists teamed up to help the U.S. establish a world and Olympic standard for the 1600-meter relay. Above, Otis Davis of Los Angeles, who set a record in the 400-meter event, has just taken the baton from Glenn Davis of Columbus, Ohio. Glenn, who won the 400-meter hurdles in 1956, proved to be faster in 1960 when he bettered his previous mark in this event.

The loosest and sweetest stride of all at Rome was the one displayed by Wilma Rudolph, right, of the U.S. women's team. The Tennessee State coed first warmed up with victories in the 100 and 200-meter sprints before catching fire to anchor the 400-meter relay quartet to triumph.

251

Glossary

AAU — Amateur Athletic Union

ANCHOR — The fourth and last position on a relay team.

ANGLE OF DELIVERY — The angle at which a missile travels in relation to the ground as it leaves the hand of the thrower.

BALL-HEEL — Referring to a contact with the ground in which the ball of the foot strikes before the heel.

BEAT THE BOARD — The vigorous striking of the take-off board in the running broad jump.

BEAT THE TRACK — The forceful contacting of the feet with the track in running.

BREAKING (start) — The act of leaving the starting marks before the official has fired the starting gun.

BREASTING THE YARN — The act of contacting the yarn with the chest at the finish of the race.

BUCK — The forward trunk bend executed by a high hurdler almost simultaneously with the spring from the ground.

BUCK FEVER — The inability to perform under tension.

CENTIPEDE RACE — A contest in which three or four athletes straddle a light pole 15 feet in length or longer, grasping it with their right hand. The legs of the contestants move in unison when running, like those of a centipede.

COLLECT — To poise or adjust oneself both mentally and physically, especially just before the takeoff in a jump or vault.

COUNTER — The upper leather part of the heel of the shoe.

CUT-DOWN — The speedy, shortened, downward leg action in the stride in preparation for striking the take-off board.

DANGER LINE — A theoretical line of demarcation between an athlete and his rival leading him in a race. Should the rival obtain a greater lead the athlete will probably lose the race.

DOUBLE FLOAT — The moment in running when both feet are off the ground.

ECHELON — The placement of runners at the beginning of a race to make certain all run an equal distance.

FREE DISTANCE — The distance gained in relay races due to the backward extension of the receiver's arm and the forward reach by the passer.

HAND HAMMOCK — The groove in the hand which supplies a natural cradle for the javelin.

JUMP-STICK-RELAY — A relay in which two or more teams line up in columns, with the athletes in each column separated an arm's length. Two members of each team grasp the ends of a six-foot stick, hold it at knee-level and sprint down their column so that in succession, each team member jumps the obstacle as it reaches him. The stick carriers are successively relieved by their teammates until each gets a turn to run with it. The team first completing a full cycle wins.

LEAD-OFF RUNNER — The athlete who runs the first section of a relay race.

MARKS — The points of contact an athlete makes with the track at the beginning of a race.

MEDLEY — A race in which the "legs" are of unequal lengths.

NCAA — National Collegiate Athletic Association.

NFSHSAA — National Federation of State High School Athletic Associations.

PACE JUDGMENT — The ability to estimate one's rate of speed.

PASSER — A runner who hands the baton to a teammate after completing his leg of a relay race.

PASSING ZONE — The 20-yard distance prescribed by relay racing rules in which the baton must be exchanged.

RECEIVER — The runner taking the baton in the passing zone in a relay race.

RECOVERY PHASE — That part of the running stride in which the leg is swinging forward into position for the oncoming drive.

RIDE — To accept in relaxed fashion the pace set by a rival who is only ahead by a few yards.

SCARECROW DANCE — A loose-jointed hopping exercise done before a race to relax the muscles.

SEMICOAST — The slight decrease in effort before reaching the take-off board.

SHUTTLE HURDLE — A relay race in which a team of hurdlers race back and forth on the hurdle course.

STOP BOARD — A curved block of wood set just outside the front edge of the shot-put circle to serve as a restraining device.

STEEPLECHASE — A race in which hurdles, hedges and water jumps are placed as hazards in the path of the runners.

TAKEOFF — The act of leaving the ground when executing a leap as in the pole vault, hurdles or high jump.

TAKE-OFF FOOT — The foot which the athlete uses to drive himself off the ground.

Bibliography

Abrahams, Harold Maurice, *Athletics*, London, Naldrett Press, 1951.

Bannister, Roger, *First Four Minutes*, London, New York, Putnam, 1955.

Bannister, Roger and Duncan, Sandy, *Oxford Pocket Book of Athletic Training*, Oxford University Press, 1957.

Bannister, Roger, *The Four Minute Mile*, New York, Dodd, Mead, 1955.

Batchelor, D. A., *A Handbook of Hammer Throwing Statistics*, Track and Field News, 1956.

Bateman, Robert, *Instructions to Young Athletes*, London, Museum Press, 1957.

Bresnahan, George Thomas, *Track and Field Athletics*, St. Louis, C. V. Mosby Co., 1956.

Canham, Don, *Field Techniques Illustrated*, New York, Ronald Press, 1952.

Canham, Don, *Track Techniques Illustrated*, New York, Ronald Press, 1952.

Cummings, Parke, *Dictionary of Sports*, New York, A. S. Barnes Co.

Doherty, John Kenneth, *Modern Track and Field*, New York, Prentice-Hall, 1955.

Kieran, John and Daley, Arthur, *The Story of the Olympic Games*, New York and Philadelphia, Lippincott, 1952.

Kozik, Frontisek, *Zatopek, The Marathon Victor*, Translated by Jean Layton, Prague, Artia, 1954.

McWhirter, Ross and Norris, *Get to Your Marks*, London, N. Kaye Co., 1951.

Menke, Frank, *Encyclopedia of Sports,* New York, A. S. Barnes, 1953.

Meyer, H. A., *Modern Athletics*, London, University Press, 1958.

Peters, J. H., *In The Long Run*, London, Cassell, 1955.

Peters, J. H., *Modern Middle and Long Distance Running*, London, N. Kaye, 1957.

Smith, George W., *All Out for the Mile*, F. Robertson Co., 1955.

Stampfl, Franz, *Franz Stampfl on Running*, MacMillan, 1955.

Weber, Jake and Rasky, Frank, *Training Olympic Champions in Track and Field*, MacMillan Co. 1951.

Index

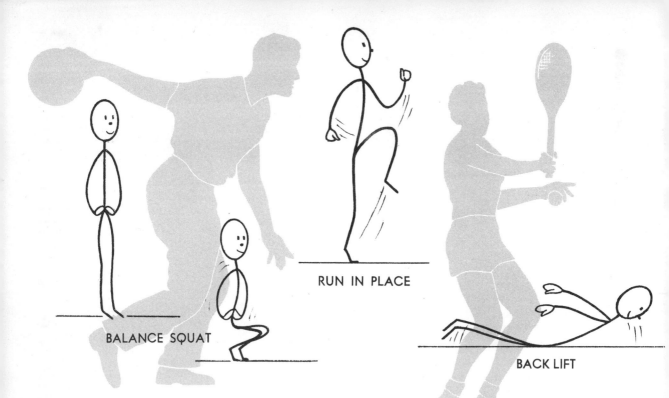

BALANCE SQUAT

RUN IN PLACE

BACK LIFT

Ten Important Daily Exercises

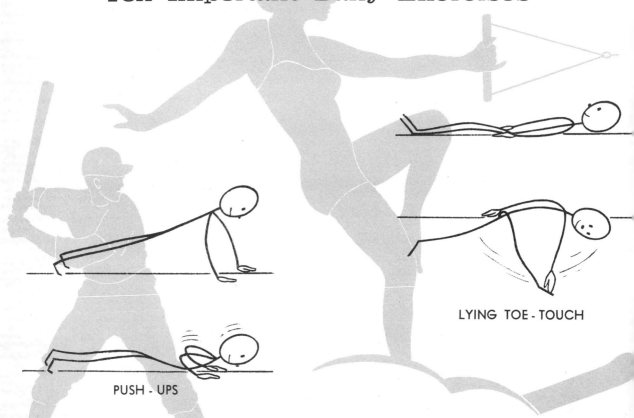

LYING TOE - TOUCH

PUSH - UPS